War Impulse Pattern

War Impulse Pattern

Primer To Not On The Map!

How To See America's War Impulse Pattern (WIP)

Wayne A. Moody

Rev. date: 11/01/2019

To order additional copies of this book, contact:
Xlibris
1-888-795-4274
www.Xlibris.com
Orders@Xlibris.com
803936

I call the cover art *Hidden Figures* in honor of the intrepid African-American women who, hidden away, were the brains behind the critical flight trajectory calculations for NASA Space missions. The cover art was executed and finalized by Jazzmin Gota on October 23, 2019.

To my dad Theodore Robert Moody Jr.,
November 4, 1930 to April 2, 2013
He left me to ponder
the mysteries of
a Rebbelid, a
Marshall Islands
Navigation
Stick and Shell Chart map.

Illustration/Photo 1. A Stick and Shell Map from the Marshall Islands

He left me
to find . . .
not a literal map of reality,
but an abstract illustration
of the hidden, secret workings underpinning reality.
He knew just what I needed to learn . . .
that there are so many different realities
simultaneously coexisting on
Earth, realities that are
NOT ON THE MAP!

On the evening of September 24, 1846, at the Berlin Observatory In Germany, Gottfried Galle and his volunteer assistant, Heinrich d'Arrest, were scanning the sky, working from calculations received the previous day from French mathematician Urbain Le Verrier. They were looking for a new planet. Just after midnight, near Verrier's coordinates, right ascension 21 h, 46 min, declination -13 deg 24 min, they found a spot out of place, to which the assistant, after consulting a recent uncirculated, cutting-edge, *star map authority, Dr. Bremiker's map of Hora XXI stated, "That star,* <u>is not on the map</u>*."*

On the pages of this book an astrological grammar rules protocol will be observed -- treating astrology with the same respect that science and other technical disciplines command. I use Liz Greene's book *The Astrological Neptune—and the Quest for Redemption*, 1996, as my authority. Greene follows in the footsteps of master astrologers like CEO Carter and Dr. Zipporah Pottenger Dobyns. In her book, the eight planets will be capitalized whenever they are mentioned. The houses will be lower case—1st house. House numbers will be arabic numbers—2nd house. Planet stations will be in caps—Direct Station and Retrograde Station. Stars referred to as Fixed Stars, Fortunate or Unfortunate in caps. Aspects will be lower case—conjunction—square. The four horoscope angles always will be capitalized—Ascendant, Midheaven, Descendant, Nadir. Their abbreviations will be all caps— ASC—MC/MH—DSC—IC. Astro*Carto*Graphy® (A*C*G) will always be capitalized and connected to the ® sign. Because specificity is a priority in this work, coordinates will be written as 35° North 22' or 76° West 56', the compass directions will always be capitalized and spelled out. Because the accuracy of horoscope times is paramount in this book, wherever possible the data has been authenticated by a recognized authority in the astrological community, the Rodden Rating system, which assigns a rating of the horoscope based upon the certitude of the date and time of birth. Since data are always volatile, the Astro-Databank is updated when new information comes to light. The data with AA, A and B ratings are fairly stable. The data with C and D ratings are the one's more likely to change with the continued upgrades to the Astro-Databank. For example, Franklin Delano Roosevelt's birth time is documented and his horoscope is Rodden Rated AA.

The *not on the map* quote will be italicized and written lower case and with spaces throughout. War Impulse Pattern (WIP), my theory, will always be capitalized.

CONTENTS

The charts and maps used in this book have been calculated using Matrix Software's Win*Star and Horizons Programs. Permission to use from Michael Erlewine.

List of Illustrations

List of Horoscopes

Horoscope Data 10. US ASCENDANT ASC ANGLE.

Horoscope Data 11. Mars-square-Neptune pattern in US horoscope.

Horoscope Data 12. Here is the 10th house placement of the Virgo Sun in the Constitution horoscope.

Horoscope 13. Of the US Constitution.

Horoscope 14. Once again, the WIP pattern in the US horoscope.

Horoscope 15. In this distilled horoscope for the Constitution you see the placement of the sun near the MIDHEAVEN angle in square (90 degrees) to Jupiter in the 7th house.

Horoscope 16. The horoscope's angles, where parans are determined, are the beginnings of the 1st, 4th, 7th, and 10th houses.

Horoscope 17. The US Neptune in relationship to Uranus—both angular.

List of Maps

Map 1. US Heartland when the country came into existence—July 4, 1776, 4:47 PM.

Map 2. The 26° Aquarius 56' moon ☾ was seen rising or ascending.

Map 3. Showing the Uranus line relationship between England and its thirteen American colonies.

Map 4. Uranus line along South Carolina coast and Charleston.

Map 5. Four angular US Mars ♂ lines.

Map 6. Four angular US Uranus ♅ lines.

Map 7. Four angular US Neptune ♆ lines.

Acknowledgments

Mitakuye Oyasin
(All Are Related)

Topping my list, like the crown of the tree of life, is my mother (September 9, 1930). If I hadn't childishly challenged her long interest in astrology, on Christmas Day 1980, I would not be an astrologer.

A select group of individuals, living and dead, stimulated my progress, offered me encouragement and directly supported the writing of this book. Their positive energy kept me energized and helped advance me along my way. Some support came from chance encounters that were magical, first-hand, once-in-my-lifetime experiences. These people were all essential to this book's creation, and so here they are, honored by naming, the living and the dead.

- Achaessa is my cheerleader, companion, co-collaborator, copyeditor, and witness to many astrological adventures and she encouraged me to blog.
- Charles Ernest Owen (CEO) Carter's book *An Introduction to Political Astrology* (1951) planted seeds, in the year of my birth, that would become part of my development and later emergence as a Mundane Astrologer
- Baris Ilhan showed my unusual ideas collegial respect, hospitality, and support in her country Turkey, where she hosted me twice.

- Icelander Julius Erinson was my reality check link from the Arctic Circle. I was *destined* to know this man and came to see this in my horoscope map relocated to Iceland.
- Lisa Furlong was the *Dartmouth Alumni Magazine* senior editor whose interview of me now stands witness to my work.
- Claire Giannini Hoffman, BofA board member, was a powerful business executive who showed me respect at great risk given her own situation and place.
- Mark Hughes talked and walked with me to his death's door, where he calmed my fears with his dignity.
- Jazz(min) Gota is an interdisciplinary, multimedia artist with a purpose and mad technical skills.
- Dr. Monica Hayes, Doc, is the sole project development editor for the entire *WIP* series of books. She was the mastermind of the multiple book approach, after closely working through many iterations and stages of the *WIP* concept. Her polymathic range of skills made her a one-stop reference source for me— mic drop!
- Illustrations the *Great Satan—Welcome to Planet Earth Journal*—Percy Franklin (1987)
- Grant Lewi, ironically a Dartmouth teacher in the 1920s, produced *Astrology for the Millions* (1940). I matriculated into Dartmouth in 1969. Lewi's book inspired my mother, who used its unconventional insights, along with Dr. Spock's *Baby Book*, to raise her children. I, the second of these children, matured to eventually appreciate astrology and specifically to embrace Lewi's system, his demonstrated ideas about Saturn's seasons of development, an actionable cycle, which can be tracked through a horoscope. I prepared my book during Saturn's *obscure phase*, in my horoscope, to be set in motion after the planet's upturn in 2018.
- Jim Lewis was among the top shelf of my astrology mentors and the creative source of the Astro*Carto*Graphy tool used throughout this book.
- Francis Toldi climbed with me, since 1981, every step of the way up the slopes of my idealistic and real mountains. He financed my first laptop, when they cost a fortune; it was critical to my work.

- And special thanks and much love to Yon Walls for living with me, loving me, and protecting my interests. I am a difficult, out-of-the-mainstream man, who is driven by a unique calling. I am grateful for that fateful call she made to the *Dartmouth Alumni Magazine* senior editor during 2013. She knew I would not have made the call.
- Michael Erlewine hired me to work at his Matrix Software Company in Big Rapids, Michigan. A Full Moon synchronized my arrival there at the right time, on the perfect stage for my initiation to computers and astrological software.

Preface

I wrote this primer to address the problem of war, the ongoing existential, perhaps now final threat to human survival in an age of artificial intelligence and drones. Can we know more, see better, and do more to avoid it? Have our philosophies about humankind, in its relationship with the Earth, evolved to the point of better, more enlightened methods and tools?

This is a book about seeing. I see the United States, the self-described leader of the free world, as having the greatest share of responsibility for preventing war in this still young twenty-first century. Our example to the world matters! The US has been locked into two of the longest wars in its history, endless wars in Afghanistan and Iraq. This book shows how they could have been anticipated, with respect to *where* and *when*, well in advance. The 35° North latitude, running through major cities in both countries, has been the key to where.

War has been the normal condition in America for more of our history then we realize. Are there better ways to address why this is so? Are there better solutions that will resolve the pressures that lead to the choice of military force? Specifically, if the option of a *just* war cannot be eliminated, then keeping it to the barest minimum is desirable. This book, and the series that follows, looks to find better intelligence into the pitfalls leading to war and suggests ways to make warfare less likely.

As has historically been the case, today's powerful leaders interact internationally, as seen in trade and security arrangements. Countries are greater than their geographic limits. They have established vital arteries to foreign lands that cannot be easily cut, once established. Interests and investments thousands of miles from their *mother* countries become stages of major geopolitical strategic concerns. In response, civilian and military interests create extensive intelligence networks.

Every innovative, informational, and technological breakthrough synchronized the rise of a new age (Bronze, Iron, Industrial, and Atomic Ages) and some famous leader heading that nation. Every nation's intelligence agencies struggle to pick the bones of every conceivable bit of knowledge for advantage. On the uncivilized stages of today's world, advantage-seeking is the name of the game and it is hotly pursued.

Perhaps if there was a more compassionate knowledge of the pressures operating in the world, knowledge of those common collective struggles for the basic guarantees of survival: the need for food, fuel, security, and water that drive conflict, we would do differently. We could ask ourselves then if the confrontations leading to war would be considerably lessened. One could hope!

My purpose is to make the common concerns we all agree upon connect with place, enhance the ability to see and appreciate more precisely, when and where the violent clash of people are likely to occur. Knowledge of this will reduce conflict. For instance, what more can be understood about US's Forward Operating Bases or Afloat Prepositioning Strategy in places like Yokosuka, Japan, or remote spots like Diego Garcia, in the heart of the Indian Ocean. These places were chosen far from American shores to prevent American citizens from experiencing the first hand effects of war.

My position is if they work, then all available resources and tools for getting at truth should be deployed toward analyzing and finding solutions to unresolved problems like those paramount climate-change-type issues of humanity. With this primer I am particularly looking at unique forms of truth, at researched intelligence, the *where* and *when* of conflict encounters over essential needs. My premise is that known in advance, intelligence might substantially reduce the possibility of war or at least reduce the destruction caused by a *just* use of military force. I offer up the credible, demonstrable insights of an ancient wisdom tool, *relocation astrology.*

Astrology philosophically and uniquely addresses issues of *when and where*, things *not on the map,* can be revealed, permitting powerful tools—thought maps—to be devised and named. I have named such a reality the *War Impulse Pattern (WIP).* The cartographic-map template laid down by the US *War Impulse Pattern* has become the baseline for my lens on US power in the world. Similarly, the 1494 Treaty of Tordesillas between Portugal and Spain, was a Papal Bull that set a demarcation line, a baseline, drawn vertically down through the center of the Atlantic Ocean, pole to pole, on the evolving maps of the times. This line on a map divided the spoils of the New World and catalyzed the emergence of ideas leading to today's international law of the sea. Ideas that led to concepts like:

1. freedom of the sea,
2. unhindered trade and travel, and
3. territorial waters.

Like this epic-mapping moment from five hundred years ago, that still shapes relationships in the world to this day, I believe that a widespread awareness of the previously, *not on the map*, US *WIP* map, particularly along its 35° North branch, as you will see as you read, can change the world.

Educate the People better, everything depends upon this!

It is my intention to demonstrate, using the US *War Impulse Pattern* (*WIP*), that these relationships, set down as lines on maps, have had had strategic value throughout the entire 242 years of US history. This includes battlefields, forts, and strategic locations that are found within the orb of these lines. As I have said, I have named the international pattern these lines create, America's *War Impulse Pattern, or WIP*. My notion of the *WIP* pattern ties together, in a stunningly logical and visual way, a distinct shape stretched across an international map—a complete picture of the *where* of US warfare. In it I can highlight the locations of most of the major American battlefields. I can show, detailed in time as well as place, *where* the US spent the people's treasure and spilled American blood. This is an extraordinary claim which I can support with documentation from public records.

I can connect the dots between the birthplaces of principal military players like George Washington and soldiers who made the final sacrifice, to battlefields and America's chief adversaries. Even monuments to the best of them, George Washington, situated along Washington DC's National Mall, can be connected to the WIP. I can connect American citizens, through their birthplaces or important life stages, to places marked by my *WIP* pattern. Conflicts, both domestic and international, fit neatly into the pattern. The *WIP* allows me a high degree of precision in predicting events. I will have more to share with you about this within these pages.

Introduction

More than three decades ago, I attended my first astrology conference and heard the following four words: There are many realities. The messenger, a silver-blue-haired woman, a member of the San Francisco Jungian society, a stranger to me, said it in passing and promptly disappeared from my life, but her once-stated words remained a force. They never left me. It was a moment of realization; something profound came into existence for me. *Great ideas, and there are many of them, serve as patterns for ideas that follow.*

What is reality? Did so many elements of ancient thought and wisdom have to be consigned to the waste bin after the reasoning of the Scientific Age took hold? We can and must resurrect and repurpose the useful.

- Must the modern science-trained technology-consuming citizens reject the reality of the mystic?
- Can one achieve a clear understanding through a symbolic language like astrology in today's world?
- Is symbolic awareness actionable?
- Is astrological reality the equal of scientific technological reality?
- Does astrology give performance like a key in a car ignition? I ask this realizing that sometimes like car ignitions, technology doesn't perform on demand.

In an atmosphere of fairness, let's look at the possibilities of astrological tools.

This book flows from first-hand research. Yes, my connecting the dots on maps will defy normal cultural beliefs about what constitutes reality and beliefs about whether one can see into the future. Readers, we look into the future all the time. Set your oven at 350 degrees and bake for three and one-half hours and voilà! You have a juicy roasted Thanksgiving turkey! The projected result is 3 1/2 hours into the future, a forecast. We can do more than this. We plan a vacation and check the weather forecasters for weather patterns during the weekend, a week away sunny and breezy! Moreover, maybe it is just right for hang gliding!

Here are more adventurous examples: I plant my spring garden and notice that on the heirloom tomato package, it says, "Expect fruit in 110 days." Sure enough, every summer, I get my tomatoes in 110 days, give or take. Then there is the fact that my daughter is expecting. Her pediatrician told her the baby is due August 19, eight months away. Yes! We forecast all the time but within limits ("i.e., limits based on accepted norms). Everyday American culture embraces the easy cycles of nature.

What are we missing? Is it Uranus, a cycle of eighty-four years, which is not in use? I use this example, dear reader, to remind you that there is more going on in the world than our own everyday experiences. If you don't accept this, then look to the mysteries surrounding NASA. Exactly what was involved in the launches of huge rockets into orbit, to the moon, in orbit around planets? These are no longer *great* secrets.

Commercial companies today are doing the work that was once the nation's greatest secrets, supported with enormous government funding and military involvement. Today, movies like *Hidden Figures* (2016) reveal the early use of *human computers* to calculate planet cycles (gravitational relationships) for scientific purposes. Today, incredibly evolved computers with artificial intelligence accomplishes that work.

In modern times, networks and systems modeled after the solar system and the circulatory system abound. We have airline routes, highway systems, shipping routes, and subway systems. All have hubs. All around us we have keyboards, wired with intricate patterns. We call them *motherboards*. They silently run our lives. Overhead in space, we have satellite systems. These have ground controls. Think GPS. All these systems and their patterns, when known, give access to their control and the possibility of directing and managing great power.

I believe that it is the genius of astrology's symbolic language component that can keep abreast of these computer science development trends that are advancing, evolving, and developing new tools. Can there be more than one purpose for these calculations and the tools they inspire? Astrologers have worked for NASA, and the military for that matter, so one should ask if there are other possible applications to make of NASA's knowledge. When a new planet is discovered, it becomes a symbolic reminder to us all that there are many realities, of which we are not yet aware and that there are many things in the world that are *not on the map!*

We comfortably predict cooking, planting, and babies but can we predict banking crises, hurricanes, or war? How often do these extreme events turn up in the average human lifespan? *This book contains my answer to these questions, particularly the question of war and demonstrates why I take an affirmative position on prediction. I can honestly say that we can forecast these concerns; the means to do so was just not on the map, until now!*

Primary sources or materials that are easily fact-checked support the events in this book. My first experience with forecasting came after a major realization in my own life, March 1985, when I, the product of a liberal arts Ivy League education, majoring in Geology, realized I had a mote in my eye. This mote dramatically changed a carefully constructed way of seeing reality that I had previously embraced. I matriculated into Dartmouth College in September 1969. The courses of study I was interested in were all in the sciences. My course load ran the spectrum from Oceanology and Plant Physiology to Mineralogy. I wanted to be a scientist!

Philosophical and religious beliefs do govern reality and the ideas in the brain frequently determine the action one initiates; thus, they govern one's destiny. I now understand what that elderly Jungian-trained woman was trying to tell wide-eyed me during my first Astrology Conference in July 1981. She said, "There are many realities." As I said before, I never saw her again, but I never forgot her words. *A reality is a fact; it's something that exists. If you are innocent or unaware of a reality, it doesn't mean it doesn't exist.* It simply means that you are inexperienced in that area, uninitiated to the facts!

On that July day, new realities began to reveal themselves to me, and I embraced changes, compelled by new realizations. In real time, I knew but did not appreciate fully, that those late July 1981 days synchronized profound astrological events, a Jupiter/Saturn Conjunction, readable and relevant to my horoscope. My initiation had begun, and the world had changed! Within a week of that experience, I climbed a 13,000 foot mountain and crossed an ice sheet in the Yosemite Wilderness with a friend—my psychopomp. For the first time I saw the starry sky in full untarnished splendor. It was a sight I had never witnessed—I was initiated now, standing in a natural staging between Earth and sky with the astrology I was growing to love writ large and tangible.

I took to that initiation. Later, in March 1985, sufficiently transfigured from my previously held beliefs, I found myself fixated on new and unfamiliar perceptions of the structure of a bank's building. I began to view the stones used to construct the building through an astrological tool. I had learned of a new technique capable of transforming astrology charts (i.e., a horoscope of the bank) and the country it served into world maps.

Once changed, such maps gradually revealed, through intuition, a new logic and passionate study, all manner of relationships previously unseen. What caught my eye almost immediately, after reviewing the bank building's horoscope and its derivative map, was the symbolic and geographic relationships of this entity to the US horoscope and its derivative map. This was an earthquake in my previously held belief system, which was solidly science-based with little taint from the metaphysical.

There is great irony in the subject bank's name, the Bank of America. The name intrigued me, so I looked more carefully at the building. Was Bank of America an arrogance naming, an advertising gimmick, or a matter of genuine suitability of those certain things happening together because they relate? In short, was this an apt name for the bank, or was it a cheat on the nation's reputation?

The bank I am referring to is San Francisco, California's Bank of America Headquarters Building at 555 California Street and Kearny. Almost every day, as part of my job duties back then (gofer for a nearby corporate law firm), I frequently went to the vast plaza of the massive bank structure. In March 1985, something compelled me to ask questions of the bank's librarian. I learned some facts about the *who*, *where*, and *what* of the building's construction and remained tethered to these facts for years.

The bank's builders constructed most of the body of the forty-four-story headquarters building from massive blocks of American Beauty Mahogany Granite from Milbank, South Dakota. The thirty-ton black granite sculpture on the main plaza came from Emmaboda, Sweden. When the US horoscope is converted into its astrology map version, the US Moon lines run to Emmaboda and Milbank. Map 1 shows the site where the bank's stone was quarried and Map 2 shows that Paris, France, the origin site of the Statue of Liberty, are all Moon-marked locations for the US. Astrologically, the Moon is a symbol of a people's security needs, food, shelter, and water. These are all the things banks make possible.

Within months of my realizations about the Bank of America, I wrote an article, *A Piece of Granite Called Transcendence*, notarized April 18, 1985, published in Eugene, OR, by *Welcome to Planet Earth*, in October 1985. The article pointed to the dawning of a partial solar eclipse in May 1985 that aligned both the American and Bank of America horoscopes. The alignment was to the most sensitive points of both horoscopes. Something was certain to synchronize with the eclipse.

I deduced from this that the bank and America would simultaneously experience some misfortune and wrote in the article, "As the 28° Taurus 50' Eclipse opposes the Saturn Station (from March 7th, 1985) and triggers the USA Moon and the Bank's Ascendant-Neptune placement, the Bank's very foundation can become liquid and flow away" (Moody, 1985). The partial solar eclipse referenced in my article appeared, synchronizing a full-blown bank equity crisis that lasted for over a year, before peaking in October 1986, with the removal of its CEO.

The genius of the astrology map was in the dots it connected and the threads they revealed. For example, the places where the bank acquired its building materials were symbolically meaningful to the US. Once again, the two locations are Milbank, South Dakota, and Emmaboda, Sweden. Flush with money from selling Alaska oil leases, the bank bought entire train loads of Milbank granite to build their headquarters. America has two of her four major Moon lines traversing the geography of these two locations.

Map 1. This map shows the astronomical relationship of the 26° Aquarius 56' moon ☾ to the US Heartland when the country came into existence—July 4, 1776, 4:47 PM.

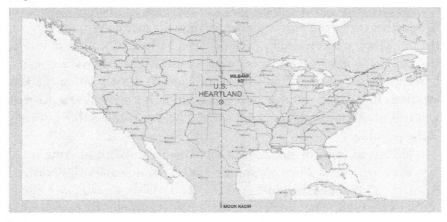

Map 2. In this map, simultaneous with events in Philadelphia, Pennsylvania, the 26° Aquarius 56' moon ☾ was seen rising or ascending.

The Moon, in a national horoscope, is a signature for the basic needs of the country's people, their food, homes, and security (C. E. O. Carter, 1951). I quickly realized that the very stone of the bank building embodied the American Moon, which was a symbol for all the peoples' security, and that what physically happened to the bank, materially was happening to the American people. It did so in a dramatic way. The Bank of America equity crisis was the *canary in the mine,* synchronizing the devastating US savings and loan (S and L) crisis that followed it, lasting a decade, across America from 1986–1995. The black granite monument, named Pacific Heritage by its sculptor, Masayuki Nagare, sitting prominently on the bank's plaza was renamed, "The Black Heart of the Banker", and it became ground 0, the target for protests against the bank.

I successfully perceived all these uncommon and unprecedented connections that were not on the map, of conventional thinking, using place and time facts from the American horoscope moment in July 1776. From my realizations of spring 1985 on, I practiced my new way of looking at events in the world; I used my growing knowledge and expertise using astrology tools to connect the dots not yet seen on the map. That is all there was to the hook, the tar baby that has gripped me these past thirty years. To date nothing has explained away, or reasoned away, this new take on seeing reality and the transcendence I felt in the original moments of discovery. Transcendence was one of the black granite stone's names, which is why I named my life-altering 1985 article, "A Piece of Granite Called Transcendence."

One more peek into the fascinating language of that new world I was navigating. America was born a Cancer entity, by beginning her national existence on July 4, 1776, when the astrological Sun, measured topically, was in the Cancer sign (13 ° Cancer 18'). The Cancer sign, ruled by the Moon, astrologically holds important defense of home, community, and country, as a top priority. Enter the traditions of the armed farmers, the minuteman patriot soldiers, militias, and standing militaries in US history.

America's armed forces, except for the air force and coast guard, have been with the country since before the signature moment of the *Declaration of Independence*: the army on June 14, 1775; the marines on November 10, 1775; the navy, October 13, 1775. Later came the coast guard on August 4, 1790; and the air force, September 18, 1947

(Graphiq, n.d.). The evolution of the United States from July 4, 1776, to the present reflects a journey, described by those defensive zeitgeist moments that were synchronized and colored by violent revolution. I focus on the events of those moments and the consequences they set off throughout the pages of this book.

I cannot repeat enough the importance of the baseline reality that is foundational to this perspective of the US. Once more, it is, "4:47 PM, on July 4th, 1776" (Guttman and Lewis, 1989, p. 281), when the Sun made its annual transit movement through the astrological sign Cancer ♋, that America was born, had its *significant moment* and emerged into concrete existence. This date and time produced a horoscope with a C Rodden Rating.

This Cancer placement is meaningful, symbolic intelligence, useful for guiding the thinking of astrologers. Besides the Sun, the US horoscope has Jupiter♃, Mercury☿, and Venus♀ symbols in Cancer. This represents 40% of the ten planets (Sun and Moon included) symbols that are placed in and read in an average horoscope. *Thus, Cancer symbolism dominates the American character. For a deep appreciation of the American temperament, all this Cancer symbolism must be unpacked, and its ruling symbol, the Moon in Aquarius ♒ sign, digested and understood. Here we see why the Bank of America bank crisis was so significant.*

Seen astrologically, the Moon rules the Sun in Cancer. The Sun ☉ is a symbol for the creative center or heart. Therefore, the Moon placement, in the US horoscope, rules the American heart, America's power center, symbolically pointing my thinking to heartfelt characteristics frequently associated with Americans. Is this useful?

o   We have a reputation as one of the major consumers of the world's resources.
o   So concerned are we about the security, wants, and needs of others, that we have proclaimed our devotion to helping others, engraved on a massive French-built statue of a woman holding a light in New York's harbor.
o   We have developed a massive Military Industrial Complex for defense.
o   America's presidents, symbolizing the country's heart are considered the most powerful men in the world.

Important Cancer planets, along with the 26° Aquarius 56' Moon, are in the 3rd, 7th, and 8th houses of the US horoscope wheel.

Horoscope 1. US horoscope containing five relevant symbols.

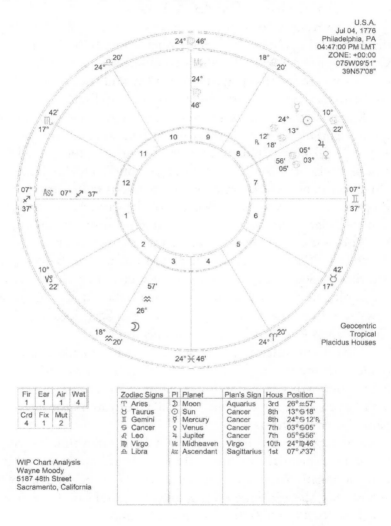

©1994 Matrix Software Big Rapids, MI

But I digress, dear reader. My story continues. In late summer 1986, I wrote two letters from Sacramento, California and had my indispensable copyeditor in San Francisco FedEx them. One was to Bank of America's Samuel Armacost, then CEO of the richest bank in the world and the other to the former board member Mrs. Claire Giannini Hoffman, the only child of the bank's founder, A. P. Giannini.

In my August 16th letter, I warned Armacost of a *Challenger-like* disaster striking the bank on September 17, 1986, or during the bank's October birthday. The Challenger Disaster had been a shockingly public catastrophe that played out to a live audience of schoolchildren. Millions of Americans witnessed the disaster on live TV and on replays.

Many of the nation's schoolchildren (children and families are quintessentially linked to the Moon) had watched the January 28, 1986, 11:39 a.m. Challenger event because of the participation of school teacher Christa McAuliffe as part of the crew (Challenger STS 551-L Accident, 1986). There was tremendous fallout to the US Space Program after this disaster. Because of the catastrophe, the US Space Shuttle Program had ceased functioning for thirty-two months.

This was the level of urgency I wanted to convey to the Bank of America CEO Armacost. What played out for the Bank of America was that on September 17, 1986, my predicted date, there was a run on the bank's stock, resulting in about two billion dollars in losses. The news headlines the next day were that the Securities and Exchange Commission was launching an investigation.

That night, after learning the news, I felt totally exposed in my home with my young family. I kept imagining a car driving past the house doing a drive-by shooting. My unsettled emotions did not permit me to celebrate that I had forecasted a major run on the world's largest bank—exact to the day!

Armacost never contacted me. Claire Giannini Hoffman, the founder's influential daughter and former board member, did. In one of two phone calls to me, after the September 17th validation of my forecast letter to her, she asked me, "What do you think I can do against a bank worth $100,000,000,000?" (That's 100 billion.)

Mrs. Hoffman suggested I contact a friend of hers, Senator Claiborne Pell of Rhode Island, because he was then chair of the Senate Foreign Relations Committee. I never did make the contact, probably because I lost my nerve. The lesson on the table for me was, if they call you, what do you give them of value? The US Security and Exchange Commission (SEC) launched an investigation. I was afraid!

The next year, nearly one year to the day, in mid-August 1987, I recovered my nerve and found my attention fixed on the Persian Gulf, along the 50° E longitude. Using threads that I had come to recognize reading the US horoscope-bank event, I issued another warning via a piece I wrote and published in Mark Lerner's *Welcome to Planet Earth Journal*, out of Eugene, Oregon. It was entitled "The Great Satan" (Moody, 1987).

In that article, I posited the astrological existence of a super-sensitive US horoscope 50° East Zone, parallel with the north-south longitude meridian, *not revealed on any other map*, running through the heart of the Persian Gulf nations. I revealed that this line was of existential importance for the United States. At that time, August 18, 1987, I wrote and published, "So what of the 50° East Zone today? Astrology reveals that this line is sensitive to transits. Any ill-timed negative occurrence [to 27° Capricorn 34'] can set off events in the countries bordering the line" (Moody, 1987).

This zone became active when Pluto crossed into late Libra, specifically 27° Libra 34', toward Scorpio, during the Iran hostage crisis of 1979. This was the time when the transiting Pluto created an astrologically significant 90-degree *aspect* relationship to the US horoscope Pluto position. A 90-degree aspect is called a square (□) and is part of the methodology used by astrologers to read a horoscope.

The square aspect signifies the probability of challenge, conflict, pressure, and in my considered opinion heralded times of great intensity of a Pluto nature for the US. Because of the near synchronicity of its February 18, 1930 discovery date, Pluto is given as signature to the scientific discoveries of the Atomic Age, of possible existential destruction. So, I saw the Gulf region as a stage where the US could experience great destructive events. Three years, four months, and twenty-eight days later, on January 15, 1991, a partial solar eclipse occurred at 25° Capricorn 20', two degrees from the planet Pluto position.

As one looks at an Astro*Carto*Graphy® map of the Persian Gulf, along the 50°° East longitude, the US horoscope Pluto marks a MIDHEAVEN reality. In astrological parlance the MIDHEAVEN (MH - MC) is where the experience is believed to happen in the open for all to witness. Research reveals that for decades, since gaining a foothold in 1931, America's military expression and commercial use of oil power in the Middle East has long been on display. Oil power was significant in guiding American policy in countries like Bahrain, Iraq, Iran, Kuwait, Oman, Saudi Arabia, UAE, and Yemen.

This 50° East longitude geographic mark is congenital, marking a strategically important part of Earth for the life of the United States.

Illustration 2. Cover of Welcome to Planet Earth—*WTPE.*

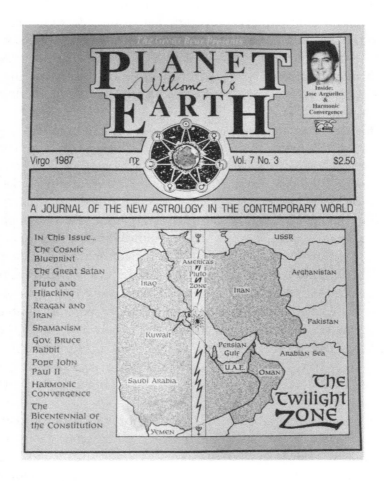

On January 17, 1991, synchronized by an annular solar eclipse to Earth, the US Pluto, which angularly and permanently marks 50° East longitude, was the stage for a half-million prepositioned American soldiers, primed for war against Iraq. My focus and timid words, published in August 1987, in Eugene, Oregon, had forecasted the *when* of war in the Persian Gulf to the day! *It would end up being the second longest war in US history.* I accurately considered both *when* and *where* using astrology tools. The operations headquarters was in Bahrain, one of the most important US naval bases in the world, precisely under the Pluto line at 50° E 36'35".

Could these astrological methods see other existential conflicts, or future wars years in advance, specific as to place and time, and not on any map? Fired up by the idea, I have worked to answer that question with this book.

Remember, dear reader, earlier in the preface, I said:

> *It is my intention to demonstrate, using the US War Impulse Pattern (WIP), that these relationships, set down as lines on maps, have had strategic value throughout the entire 242 years of US history. This includes battlefield after battlefield, fort after fort, strategic location after strategic location that are found within the orb of these lines. I have named the international pattern these lines create, America's War Impulse Pattern or WIP. My notion of the WIP pattern ties together, in a stunningly logical and visual way, a distinct shape stretched across an international map—a complete picture of the where of US warfare. In it I can highlight the locations of most of the major American battlefields. I can show, detailed in time as well as place, where the US spent the people's treasure and spilled American blood. This is an extraordinary claim which I can support with documentation from public records.*

> *I can connect the dots between the birthplaces of principal military players like George Washington and soldiers who made the great sacrifice, to battlefields and America's chief adversaries. I can connect them, through their birthplaces or important life stages, to places marked by my WIP*

pattern. Conflicts, both domestic and international, fit neatly into the pattern. The *WIP* allows me a high degree of precision in predicting events. I will have more to share with you about this within these pages.

America's military and citizen travelers alike also have different congenitally established spatial sensitivities to the Earth's geography. Specific people, astrologically identified in the vetting, have the possibility of each being deployed by the US government, like acupuncture needles serving the nation for use on America's immense military presence in its world body. I mean the world *body* in the sense that we are, from Albert Einstein, all "a part of the whole called by us 'the universe', a part limited in time and space. He experiences himself, his thoughts and feelings, as something separate from the rest—a kind of optical illusion of consciousness" (Einstein, 1972).

Astrology shows that select American citizens, in service to the US, bring a hidden astrological component with the service they bring to a place. Every person, even a foreign-born American who immigrated, is born with unique horoscope connections around the Earth. Take for example America's 188 ambassadors (as of May 25, 2017) to the world's "Total count of independent states: 195" foreign capitals, the US acknowledges (US Department of State, Fact Sheet, 2017). An example follows that demonstrates the importance of knowing what that hidden astrological signature for an individual says that is *not revealed on the map* by conventional vetting methods.

The American ambassador to Iraq April Glaspie met with Saddam Hussein at the Presidential Palace, in Baghdad, Iraq, on July 25, 1990, just eight days before Iraq invaded Kuwait. On that occasion, she is alleged to have spoken fateful words that many contend triggered Hussein's invasion of Kuwait. She is credited with saying, "We have no opinion on your Arab-Arab conflicts, such as your dispute with Kuwait. Secretary Baker has directed me to emphasize the instruction, first given to Iraq in the 1960's, that the Kuwait issue is not associated with America." About the words attributed to her during her meeting with Saddam, Ambassador Glaspie says this, "This version was invented by Tarek Aziz. After all Tarek was a master of words as a previous Minister of Information and editor of a newspaper."

US Ambassador Glaspie is accused of unwittingly lighting a match that ignited America's first war against Iraq. The war involved the US directly, no longer covertly, in the instability that rages to this day now nearly twenty-nine years on through the whole of the Middle East. America's war experience in Iraq is one of the two longest wars in US history.

Why this American? Does her birthdate—April 26, 1942, place—Vancouver, British Columbia, Canada, and time—unknown, show something, *not on the map*? Do any of the vital numbers, common in any bio on her, her driver's license, or her passport, hold any more insight into why she ended up as a critical American player on that Iraqi stage at that fateful moment in history—July 25, 1990?

Her birth date on these documents do hold some revelations. I do not have a Rodden-Rated birth time for Glaspie, but in an untimed horoscope, compared to the US *WIP*, there are tight connections between her Taurus Sun-sign ruler Venus, at 19°–20° Pisces, forming an important opposition and squares to the WIP planets. She also has her Jupiter, at 20° Gemini + on the US *WIP* Mars placement at 21° Gemini 22', squaring the US Neptune at 22° Virgo 25'. Astrologically, the reason the moment Ambassador Glaspie and President Hussein met on July 25th, 1990, was so pregnant with meaning is seen in the transits of that day.

Numbers matter. Transiting Mars had just crossed Glaspie's 5–6° Taurus Sun placement in the days just prior to her meeting with Saddam Hussein. Simply stated, when you add 45°, an astrological semi-square aspect indicating stress to her Sun placement, you get 20°–21° Gemini the US WIP Mars. A XX Rodden-Rated horoscope gives 7°–8° Taurus as Hussein's birth Sun position. He is said to have been born on April 28, to Glaspie's April 26th. By September 2, 1990, transiting Mars had moved to enter Gemini and after a long period of retrograde and direct movements, Mars would realize its 114th US Mars Return on March 16, 1991. The Gulf War ended February 28, 1991. Mars Return events in the US horoscope have been very important barometers of war in US military history.

Finally, and what seems to me an extremely relevant fact, the US Mars Return crossed President George H. W. Bush's Rodden-Rated AA Sun position at 21° Gemini 19'. This is important because Glaspie answered to Bush. Her birth Sun symbolizing her authority was in conflict with his. President George H. W. Bush, the youngest naval pilot in WWII, a war hero, was born with a horoscope made for the 1991 American war in the Persian Gulf. His horoscope plugged tightly into the US *WIP*, into the Iraqi geographic heartland, along its 35° North latitude branch, where he as US Commander-in-Chief, conducted a major air—Gemini—war, beginning with the largest airlift in history. It should not surprise us that US Mars Returns also timed the beginning of the US War with Mexico, the Civil War, and WWII.

Back to Ambassador Glaspie. The geographical numbers story for this significant ambassador in US history are that she was born on April 26, 1942, in Vancouver, British Columbia, Canada. Does her birth in the US-relocated horoscope to Vancouver matter or show something *not on the map*? America's relocated horoscope to Vancouver has 4° Leo 54' at the Midheaven Angle, with the North Node symbolizing America's *schedule for growth into the future* (☊) nearby at 7° Leo 36'. Add 45 degrees to the US North Node and you get 22° Virgo 36', nearly the WIP Neptune placement at 22° Virgo 25'. Can we further unpack information from these uncommon numbers? Do any of these numbers hold any more insight into why she ended up that critical American player on that Iraq stage at that fateful moment in history—July 25, 1990?

Is the US using the tools that can best measure and sort out these critical people's appropriate service, worth, and value to the nation? During my long years of research, I have noticed that a number of public officials in high office are not disclosing their birth dates and places in their biographies.

Instructions to the Reader

Dear reader,

You are about to travel the Earth in what may be an unfamiliar vehicle, Astrology. As you begin reading, you will learn about the tools and the ideas you will need to support you on your journey. Your journey and destination do not appear on any conventional map, so I will put it on a map for you. You will learn about new and unusual annotations on this map.

There are four main ideas illustrated: synchronicity, symbolism, a collective mind, and angular relationships of 0 (☌), 90 (□), and 180 (☍) degrees, between select planets and the Earth, experienced like sunrise, noon, and sunset, demonstrated through amazing new maps. If you are turning the pages of this book, I am guessing that you have the requisite curiosity and faith tools. Curiosity gets you to open yourself to the many realities that exist. Faith lets you hold on to your own moorings when you are rocked by something awesome and not on the map!

So

- you need to be curious enough to try,
- you need to try to believe,
- you need to believe in the new skills, and
- you need to trust and use this unique set of skills.

The first tool deals with TIME.

The time protocol used in the world is universal. In the business community, for the military, time measure has just one baseline. It used to be set in Greenwich, United Kingdom from 1884 until the 1980s. In today's computer-driven world, it is increasingly set by what is called the Network Time Protocol (NTP), the synchronization of computer clocks. Time today goes everywhere you do. It's in your pocket on your smartphone. Everything is part of an awesomely choreographed dance of relationship, involved in a flow of natural time.

New applications of time, seen astrologically, will further expand knowledge. It will give you the eyes to see extraordinary relationships, using dotted lines between events happening in the sky and simultaneously on Earth, events that are synchronistic, profound connections, and they are not identified as being causally related.

The second tool is *SYMBOLISM*.

You will learn to appreciate subtle ideals, their hidden qualities, juxtapositions, relationships and skillfully unpack deeper layers of meanings and values at play in the world through the second tool.

Symbolism is a universal language, a set of coded, complex ideals that can reveal deep underlying patterns and states of mind. Once mastered symbols can serve to put a common language to the meaning of events globally. Symbols connect together in correspondences, which allow quick associations to be made. You will learn to read expanded levels of meanings in established facts and natural objects, around the Earth, using symbolic lines. Koestler taught us that, "Certain things like to happen together!"

The third is the COLLECTIVE-MIND tool.

> You will philosophically see yourself more connected (again correspondences), as part of a great whole, while still operating as an individual but within the context of a dizzying array of larger groups—families, communities, states, nations, races, and species. This perspective is the tool that will show you that you have a great deal in common with the rest of the geographic world.

The fourth tool is CARTOGRAPHY.

> Cartography, according to *Merriam-Webster,* means "the science or practice of drawing maps" which means measuring Earth's ground realities. When you add Astro, you make measurements between the realities in the sky (astro means celestial object or star) and the Earth, producing a collection of highly specialized maps. These maps feature lines conveying the concept of angular relationships, measured as 0, 90, or 180-degree alignments between Earth and sky, as seen by astrology.

These Astro*Carto*Graphy® (A*C*G) Maps are keys that provide the means to give qualitative and quantitative voices to the meanings of our relationships to Earth's geography. Angularity is an ephemeral condition resulting from the Earth's daily and yearly cyclical movements around the Sun, movement also relative to other planetary bodies. These movements symbolize the passage of natural time (our day, month, and year cycles), which fall under the first tool above TIME and is the foundation of this book's astrological journeying. *I believe the way you experience and see the world will change when you learn to manage—through time, travel or outreach—your angular relationships to Earth, with a knowledge of planet movements in time, transiting through your horoscope or as lines on maps.*

As you travel the Earth, directly, indirectly, or vicariously through information, media, or trade goods,

- you will learn to be curious about where personally meaningful dots of geography, representing places marked with unique angular emphasis, if not distinction, occurred in your birth moment.
- you will be initiated into how to connect dots of similar value to produce lines, a baseline of any cartography tool.
- you will start using such a cartography map, informed by astrologically dictated lines, your symbolically informed journey will join with and emphasize the conventional markings—the latitude and longitude measurements while assigning meanings *not on the map* of ordinary thinking.
- you will see how you relate to Earth's 195-odd distant nations, even to their names, will be seen as rational, guided by meaningful lines, and no longer coincidental!
- you will see startling depths of purposefulness to your reaching out to or physically relocating to particular lines, at particular times, over thousands of miles.
- you will reflect back upon your life and realize that even your pre-Astro*Carto*Graphy ® map-consciousness experiences will take on new meaning.

Recapping:

Maps can be annotated with lines representing planets, seen in their guise as astrological archetypes, frozen into patterns of relationships in your, or some entity's birth-moment horoscope. Using these mapped planet patterns, you can cultivate the ability to see attention-grabbing, geographically fixed places, *not on the map*, of conventional map tools. If it is your own horoscope, then you will see that which is congenital to your life story, dovetailing with instinctual interest all along the way.

I *am asking you to cultivate a belief in symbolic abstractions in astrologically annotated map representations, realizing that while they seem but symbols, pondering them can inspire, prod, or stimulate choices.* This means you can embrace ideals represented by symbols, as being tangible and actionable, not some movie fiction with all the action on the screen while you sit passively. *The genius of astrology is its ability to time action and set the stage in preparation for its season.*

- *I ask that you cultivate your skill at pattern recognition so that you can make connections between the facts that make up history and symbolism. Astrology builds its stories, adhering to the unalterable facts of the when and where of things. One cannot easily corrupt place and time facts in history. You are left to tease out the why, the symbolic value of these facts.*
- *I am going to teach you how to appreciate and cultivate new ideals through new vocabulary.*
- *You will learn how to work at understanding unfamiliar concepts like, Astro*Carto*Graphy® (A*C*G) square aspect, and Zeitgeist.*

My interest here is to address those collective realities, that we are meant to share, as part of the enfranchised citizens of the United States. These include common prosperity, domestic security, education, peacetime pursuit of happiness, and war. No collective experience is more profound than war.

I address that reality looking for what is not on the map, *something not seen using conventional knowledge systems. There are, in the interactions between the horoscope of the US and each of us, as individuals, great mysteries. Our individual contributions and collective action built and continue to build the country, writing its history.*

Chapter 1

The Traditional Astrological Mundane Meanings for Mars ♂, Uranus ♅, and Neptune ♆

From 20ᵀᴴ Century Astrologers H. S. Green, C. E. O. Carter to Researcher Rex E. Bills

As the heading states, we are astrologically concerned here with the meanings of three planets. We look at the concrete reality of them in terms of current commonly realized quantifiable facts, as well as with the belief in them by the culture, the qualitatively symbolic astrological realities. Often reality and symbol are joined at the hip synchronistically. In a sense, there is a great irony playing out here because there was a time, 1781 and 1846, when both astronomically and astrologically, two of our three *WIP* planets, Uranus and Neptune, didn't even exist in the minds and languages of human beings. They were literally and physically *not on the map*!

Horoscope 2. The C Rodden Rated US horoscope, set for July 4, 4:47 p.m., 1776, on staging in Philadelphia, Pennsylvania.

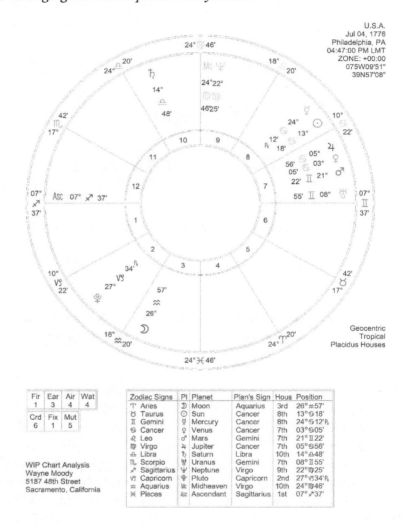

U.S.A.
Jul 04, 1776
Philadelphia, PA
04:47:00 PM LMT
ZONE: +00:00
075W09'51"
39N57'08"

Geocentric
Tropical
Placidus Houses

Fir	Ear	Air	Wat
1	3	4	4

Crd	Fix	Mut
6	1	5

WIP Chart Analysis
Wayne Moody
5187 48th Street
Sacramento, California

	Zodiac Signs	Pl	Planet	Plan's Sign	Hous	Position
♈	Aries	☽	Moon	Aquarius	3rd	26°♒57'
♉	Taurus	☉	Sun	Cancer	8th	13°♋18'
♊	Gemini	☿	Mercury	Cancer	8th	24°♋12'℞
♋	Cancer	♀	Venus	Cancer	7th	03°♋05'
♌	Leo	♂	Mars	Gemini	7th	21°♊22'
♍	Virgo	♃	Jupiter	Cancer	7th	05°♋56'
♎	Libra	♄	Saturn	Libra	10th	14°♎48'
♏	Scorpio	♅	Uranus	Gemini	7th	08°♊55'
♐	Sagittarius	♆	Neptune	Virgo	9th	22°♍25'
♑	Capricorn	♇	Pluto	Capricorn	2nd	27°♑34'℞
♒	Aquarius	Mc	Midheaven	Virgo	10th	24°♍46'
♓	Pisces	Asc	Ascendant	Sagittarius	1st	07°♐37'

Novice 2 Wheel

KEY WIP BRANCHES: 35° NORTH & SOUTH ~ 6° NORTH & SOUTH
10° EAST ~ 103° EAST ~ 77° WEST ~ 169° WEST ~ 3° WEST

Horoscope 3. The same US horoscope distilled to just three featured planets: Mars ♂, Uranus ♅, and Neptune Ψ, and the relationships (aspects—degree separation) between them.

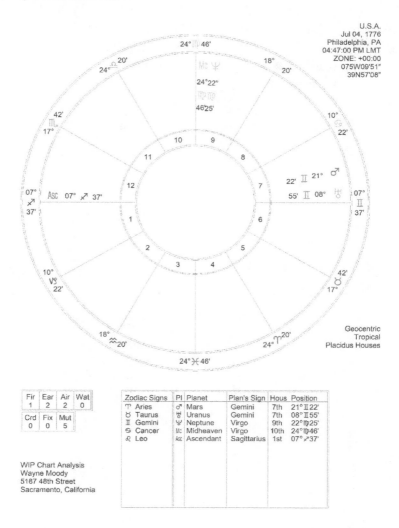

| U.S.A. |
| Jul 04, 1776 |
| Philadelphia, PA |
| 04:47:00 PM LMT |
| ZONE: +00:00 |
| 075W09'51" |
| 39N57'08" |

Geocentric
Tropical
Placidus Houses

Fir	Ear	Air	Wat
1	2	2	0

Crd	Fix	Mut
0	0	5

Zodiac Signs		Pl	Planet	Plan's Sign	Hous	Position
♈	Aries	♂	Mars	Gemini	7th	21° Ⅱ 22'
♉	Taurus	♅	Uranus	Gemini	7th	08° Ⅱ 55'
Ⅱ	Gemini	Ψ	Neptune	Virgo	9th	22° ♍ 25'
♋	Cancer	Mc	Midheaven	Virgo	10th	24° ♍ 46'
♌	Leo	Asc	Ascendant	Sagittarius	1st	07° ♐ 37'

WIP Chart Analysis
Wayne Moody
5187 48th Street
Sacramento, California

©1994 Matrix Software Big Rapids, MI

Novice 2 Wheel

KEY WIP BRANCHES: 35° NORTH & SOUTH ~ 6° NORTH & SOUTH
10° EAST ~ 103° EAST ~ 77° WEST ~ 169° WEST ~ 3° WEST

MARS ♂ 21° GEMINI 22' ♂ URANUS ♅ 8° GEMINI 55' □ NEPTUNE ♆ 22° VIRGO 25'

Data 1. Spotlighting the Mars square Neptune.

Neptune is the trident-shaped symbol near the vertical line marking the 10th house of the horoscope. Neptune is in the 9th house of the horoscope. The line is called the *Midheaven* (MH/Mc) angle. Neptune is a near perfect quarter circle (90°) from Mars— the circle with the arrow protruding from it. This relationship of Mars to Neptune is called a square (□) aspect and reads as constant conflict, pressure, or tension.

♆ | Neptune | Virgo | 9th | 22°♍25' |

U.S.A.
Jul 04, 1776
Philadelphia, PA
04:47:00 PM LMT
ZONE: +00:00
075W09'51"
39N57'08"

4°♍46'

18°
20'
♆
22°
♍
25'
10°
22'
) ☽
9
8
♂ 21° Ⅱ 22'
7
07°
Ⅱ
37'
6

♂ | Mars | Gemini | 7th | 21°Ⅱ22'

KEY WIP BRANCHES: 35° NORTH & SOUTH ~ 6° NORTH & SOUTH
10° EAST ~ 103° EAST ~ 77° WEST ~ 169° WEST ~ 3° WEST

Dear reader, the following are common definitions that have been widely circulated for upwards of one hundred years in the astrological English-speaking world. They are definitions for the important WIP planets, the astrological Mars, Uranus, and Neptune, which will be emphasized throughout this book. These definitions have been tested by the works of noted authorities in recent time. I hope you will find these valuable definitions to be a helpful reference throughout your reading journey.

Astrologer H. S. Green

These first correspondences and definitions of Mars, Uranus, and Neptune are from Astrologer H. S. Green, born September 16, 1861, 3:00 a.m. His birth data has a Rodden Rating of C. Green's *Mundane Astrology* was published in the early 1900s.

Mars ♂

Green said Mars is the planet of desire and aversion; it impels to action for the sake of securing the object of desire and driving away the object of aversion; and [*sic*] in doing this it imparts energy and activity to the sign and house in which it is placed . . . It is the planet of war, of soldiers, sailors, agitators, rebels, violent criminals, and of all who dispute and contend; [*sic*] it also indicates surgeons, engineers, and workers in iron, and rules fires, poisons, and crimes of violence. Mars rules the sword in the constellation Orion's belt.

Uranus ♅

Green observed that the planet Uranus seems to stand for people who exercise power and authority in the country, from the Monarch downward, and for corresponding persons in smaller departments of national life . . . In common with Mercury it has something to do with railways, science, electricity, and perhaps aviation.

Neptune ♆

For Green Neptune seems to represent democratic political movements, the fluctuations of popular opinion, the influence and interests of the people, popular institutions, perhaps hospitals and charities . . . When afflicted, it causes collapse, downfall, a chaotic condition of affairs, instability, scandal, drunkenness, dishonesty, deception, and various forms of crime and vice.

Mars ♂

Mars denotes soldiers, surgeons, noted military and naval men, war, disputes, fire and incendiarism.

Uranus ♅

Uranus has special influence over railroads, societies and associations, gas and water companies, civic bodies, strikes, rioting, and the like. Aerial navigation and scientific discoveries come also under this planet's rule, also explosions, anarchy, and nihilism.

Neptune ♆

Neptune rules socialism, suffragettes, the smart set, plots, sedition, fraud and swindling, all illicit undertakings, bogus companies, and all the lower and more degrading forms of vice and wickedness.

Astrologer C. E. O. Carter

The following definitions are C. E. O. Carter's. He was born January 31, 1887, 11:01 p.m. Carter's birth data has a Rodden Rating of A. Carter's *An Introduction to Political Astrology* was published by L. H. Fowler in 1951. Here we find his take on the same three astrological symbols making up the US WIP. As an astrologer, Carter was an eyewitness to the *Weltgeist* (World Spirit of the Times) and efforts by the astrologers to forecast the times that produced WWII. He wrote, "In mundane work many factors are involved. More indeed, often enough, for any one person to be able to comprehend in his mind [*sic*]. Yet the attempt must be made."

In his groundbreaking, *An Introduction to Political Astrology*, he writes:

Mars ♂

> Carter wrote that Mars rules the armed forces and also all trades that minister to these; it has much to do with engineering."

Uranus ♅

> Uranus, in Carter's mind, seems also to have kinship with the administrative officers of the State and their functions . . . Probably it also rules power on the physical plane-dynamos and all power-generators. It is connected with electricity."

Neptune ♆

> Carter wrote, Neptune is related to Pisces and the 12th house . . . having affinity with hospitals and all charitable institutions and organizations, things that exist to help others. It has relation to the mercantile marine and the Navy.

Researcher—Rex E. Bills

In the late twentieth century, researcher Rex E. Bills organized tables of the ancient astrology definitions with new evolved and modernized understandings that had come into the field. In his book, The *Rulership Book – A Directory of Astrological Correspondences* (Bills, 1971), he set down the best understanding of astrological symbols: the houses, signs, and the planets. He listed corresponding values for the three planets just given for a modern reading audience. Throughout this book are references to correspondences (things that have close similarities or equivalences). I use them to explore the US pattern of war. They go far in assisting astrologers in their efforts to paint reality, as they read different horoscopes, use their correspondence reasoning and put what is seen marked by lines from their derivative maps into context.

From Bills' book, a common reference source found in many professional astrologers' libraries, I grab from lists, select examples from pages 215–227 for Mars, 265–280 for Uranus, and 281–297 for Neptune. Keep in mind that language has a life. Words can be born and die. Language is constantly evolving by culture, through individual people, innovation, national experience, and purpose and by the general neologic processes of naming the world anew.

The establishment of the *Webster* dictionary, around the time of the establishment of the US Constitution, was a deliberate act of nationalizing the common language. The process is ongoing—it never stops. Realizing and listing correspondences never stops. For example, all the words descriptive of the Atomic Age (1945) and of the Personal Computer Age (1977) are relatively recent additions as players in world history. Indeed, all the worlds a stage.

Just ten years ago (2007), there was no iPhone! By August 2017 1.2 billion iPhones had been sold. Where would the iPhone appear on an updated Bills's list, under Mercury? Uranus? Here are some of Bills's modern correspondences for Mars.

From the pages of his book, Bills listed these words as corresponding with Mars: "*Aggressors, ammunition, armaments, armament makers, arsenals, artillery, battleships, battlefields, blood, bravery, brutality, bullets, cannons, casualties, cemetery workers, conflict, deaths, enemies, firearms, (flags), glory in battle, guns-gunners-gun makers and dealers, and madness*" (*Bills, 1971, pp. 215–221*). We can relate to these words because American history, beginning long before 1776, is written with them. But today's wars have new words like IEDS and drones; this new vocabulary emerged after Bills, thus its not contained in his listings.

It has been nearly fifty years since Bills published his book. We must continually and carefully upgrade these astrological correspondence tables if we are to keep our grip on the consensus reality accurate and stay at the forefront of events. All of those Mars correspondences, just listed, explicitly name specific details of war.

They are part of "those things that like to happen together" that are celebrated in the US version of the Roman temples of war. During the actual time of war, these are the words that describe synchronicities between Earth and sky. Where war happens for the US, astrological synchronicities to Mars can be recognized and tracked in horoscopes and maps. They can be made clear and actionable, using correspondence language. If said another way, the correspondences for Mars all constitute the vocabulary of war. In modern warfare, new concepts, innovations, and technologies continually add fresh new language to Bill's correspondence tables. Think drones.

It is also important to keep continuity with past astrological wisdom. Dr. J. Lee Lehman sets the record out in her 1992 book *The Book of Rulerships*. While avoiding compiling correspondence for the modern planets Uranus, Neptune, and Pluto, she thoroughly documents the long-held correspondence of Mars to war.

She cites back to Ptolemy's, the *Greek*, *Tetrabiblios* from the AD 2 century and moves up through centuries of agreement with Arab al-Biruni (AD 973–1048), during Medieval times. From deep antiquity, she maintains the thread of astrologers to the dawning of the Scientific Age: Frenchman Claude Dariot (1533–1594), Englishmen William Lilly (1602–1681), Nicholas Culpeper (1616–1654), John Gadbury (1627–1704), Richard Saunders (1613–1692), William Ramesey (1626–1676?), and John Partridge (1644–1714).

They each make the connection between war and its elements. Looking back in time starting from Ptolemy's writings connecting Mars with iron, sudden deaths, and war, we see that subsequent astrologers saw Mars connected to commanding officers. Corresponding connections continued down through the ages to technologically improved weapons like sniper-rifles.

It is important to note the evolution of astrological thinking as it relates to war. I cannot overstate the importance of practicing astrologers' task to unabashedly add new language to advance the ancient historical record. Their work enriches the field of understanding beyond Rex E. Bills's (1971), and Dr. Lehman's (1992) *Rulerships* lists.

Many new expressions of Mars have entered the languages of the world since 1992 and Dr. Lehman's groundbreaking list of *Rulership*.

KEY WIP BRANCHES: 35° NORTH & SOUTH ~ 6° NORTH & SOUTH
10° EAST ~ 103° EAST ~ 77° WEST ~ 169° WEST ~ 3° WEST

For example, by 2015, there was an awareness of the massive use of armor-piercing projectiles, under Mars-marked places, by the US. These were projectiles using the very dense *depleted uranium* in bullets and bombs.

Depleted uranium is an example of newly coined language with specific meaning. It is a new material that because of its great density, it can also be used for protection and is sandwiched between tank armor to give it massive strength. In another example of new language related to Mars and war, the escalating use of military *drones* and firing of *GPS-guided missiles* are twenty-first-century additions to the English language.

So are *night-vision goggles* and *improvised explosive devices*—the unconventional IED—popularized and commonly used in Iraq during the 2003–2014 war. *Rest assured that the Iraqis have added their own word for this development to their language. When an astrologer looks at an active Mars line, marking a battlefield in Iraq and 1,000 anti-tank missiles arrive in the hot war zone from the US, it is the American astrological Mars arriving. The US is the world's largest arms merchant.*

One must shudder at the thought of what secret weapons are being stockpiled for future American wars.

Twenty-First-Century Uranus ♅—Revolution by People and Administration of Power for People

Uranus correspondences are more complex than those of Mars, less objective, and more about ideals. Star Wars was a Uranian ideal of war. The new Space Force is Uranian. Near the beginning of Bills's Uranus listings is *"ability, one's constructive and mechanical."* The *WIP* Mars spurs construction and mechanical innovation in many technologies to produce weapons of war and all that supports military forces. Some Uranus correspondences listed by Bills are *"advanced thought, (adversaries), aerial navigation, aeronautic apparatus, airmen, airplanes-airships, airplane mechanics, ammunition, announcers-radio and television, bombs-bombers, (boundary lines), (bridge builders), bullets, clocks"* (Bills, 1971, pp. 265–267).

This is just a brief sample of the correspondence language used for Uranus that is found in war. It is worth repeating here that in the US horoscope, this Uranus symbol joins with the Mars language, just laid out, to describe the military prowess of the US, fighting in the air through its history. Mars and Uranus values must work in some amicable way together, because aspect-wise, 13 degrees apart in the horoscope on an angle, their closeness makes them a formidable pair. An example of this would be the US control and use of Global Positioning System (GPS) in war.

Again, as in any two-legged sack race, the pair must cooperate to attain a common goal. This is the challenge of Mars and Uranus, expressing together in Gemini's realm of ideas. This makes US procurement of advanced technology a tightrope act. Projects are frequently over budget, buggy and late. Near the end of Bills's listing of Uranus correspondences is *"unforeseen, the."* We live in times that warrant a need to revisit the notion of anticipating unforeseen events because *Uranus is part of an instinct to know something, without knowing why.*

It was said that events leading to 9/11 were unforeseen! Yet, in the worldview of astrology, this was not the case. Several astrologers, myself included, were buzzing around the *when*; some had a sense of the reclusive *where. Forecasting two and a half years out, I was within tens of miles and off by 44 days.*

A few astrologers nailed the event, forecasting the *when, where,* as well as, *the what* (specifically citing airplanes used as weapons of attack) of the historic event. Latinist medieval scholar and astrologer Robert Zoller predicted 9/11 two years in advance of the event.

Using Medieval Astrology, Robert Zoller:

1. predicted the events of 9/11
2. published those predictions over two years beforehand
3. specifically stated that the attack would be by Islamic fundamentalists on US soil
4. stated that it would occur September 2001
5. specifically named Bin Laden
6. stated that the House of Bush would be responsible for the mismanagement of the disaster

Historian Benson Bobrick writes about Zoller (aptly enough), a specialist in Arabic astrology, that he saw the attack of September 11 coming almost as clear as day. His prediction unfolded in a series of forecasts, each one more sharply focused than the last. A lowly but capable astrological scholar poring over a handful of tell-tale charts—using the mundane predictive methods of Ptolemy, Masha'allah, Abu Ma'shar and Bonatti—knew more about what was likely to happen that day than all the intelligence experts combined in the FBI and CIA (Bobrick, 2005). Interestingly, on page 53 of *The Fated Sky*, this is quoted from Ptolemy, "It is not possible that particular forms of events should be declared by any person, however scientific; since the understanding conceives only a certain general idea of some sensible event, and not its particular form." Keep up on your correspondences astrologers!

Relocation techniques have been around since before the time of the medieval astrologers like John Dee (1527–1609), who advised Queen Elizabeth I of England. Dee was an expert in navigation, at a time when the Age of Exploration was just beginning to fill in the geographic maps of the Earth. *Understand that in my privileged, modern, computer-informed view, it would take a roomful of medieval astrologers their entire lifetimes to plot all the geographic dots that it takes to make a comprehensive map, such as I regularly use, one with a straight line wrapping the whole Earth at 35° North latitude. Today the US WIP is generated in seconds using specialized software.*

In my opinion, what distinguishes my skills from the medievalist is the added factual, actionable completeness of my maps, which align and assign US planet lines symbolism geographically, revealing a vast international pattern, all war related. My WIP map tool is made up of a number of these straight lines, which combine to form a vast pattern covering huge swaths of the Earth. I repeat, today's computer enhancements to astrology allow those calculations to be made in seconds, providing me, a skilled reader, a near immediate intuitive flash and gestalt from an awesome perspective, that can be measured and studied in a handheld map.

It is the information of a lifetime of calculations, gathered in one grand gestalt. It is actionable. If an informed US leadership, one symbolized in the horoscope by Neptune in the 9th House on MIDHEAVEN, were to give guidance and parental pressure informed by tools like the WIP, then the impulse to act on the part of the civilian public will be more enlightened, ethical, and much-better directed.

Since I am trained to read this map tool, in ways meaningful to modern life in a global world, *I have a considerable mapping advantage over the ancient master astrologers. What I need to do, with greater skill, is see the general idea of Mars/Uranus in Gemini symbolism, and then dare to imagine the 9/11 airplane weapon in the hands of a hostile ideology like Al-Qaeda and its leadership. I must be sensitive to a broad spectrum of events expressing in the boundaries of the WIP, but not to any particular form, realizing them as the many facets of a symbol, constantly changing their faces in their widespread manifestations.*

The Mars-Neptune-Uranus trio is an army rest and recreation (liquor and sex) stage in one place and an arms-contract manufacturing plant in another and bloody battlefield in yet another. In the eighteen years since 9/11, the US 7th House, Mars/Uranus in Gemini, has morphed into forms hard to imagine: cyber technologies, robotics, Terminal High Altitude Area Defense (THAAD), unmanned Predator Drones, and other secret air technologies are still coming off drafting boards.

Twenty-First-Century Neptune ♆—Collective Power, Merchant Shipping, Naval Forces, and Organizations Meant to Help Others

Neptune is less objectifiable than Mars or Uranus. It is more abstract, misty, and difficult to quantify materially. Gases, which are difficult to detect, are listed by Bills as corresponding with Neptune and Pisces, the sign it rules.

In its 9th house placement in the US horoscope, Neptune is about the collective spirit of the people, that iconic idealism of "We the People." Neptune represents that collective, public spirit-power of the masses, energy that can be tapped to drive great endeavors, like the American Revolution. Like the ocean it has long symbolized, Neptune corresponds with the vast repositories and wave flows of the human culture. One can be lifted up or drowned in them.

Many times, the realized cultural values are pure glamor—the Pepsi Generation, for example! At other times, Neptune values color the Zeitgeist seen in the run-up to 1848 and Communism, a time which synchronized with Neptune's actual discovery on September 23, 1846, at 25° Aquarius 54' placement, moving retrograde. There is also the Hippie Summer of Love Zeitgeist of 1967, when major astrological events, one a Full Moon at 26° Aquarius 24', aligned to the US 1776

Moon position—26° Aquarius 56'. Some Neptune correspondences from Bills are

> *addicts, alcohol-alcoholism-alcoholic beverages, cigars-cigarettes, cinemas, circumnavigation, clandestine, clouds, coffee, drugs, gasoline, gelatin, habit-forming drugs, harbors-harbors for ships, hidden forces, hospitals-hospitalization-hospital worker, hypodermic needles, lenses, lubrication, magnets, (magnification), (medicines), meerschaum, motion pictures, music-cultural, navies-naval men and officers-naval affairs, navigation-navigators, (nursing-nurses), submarines* (Bills, 1971, pp.281–295).

These are all things commonly known in America today. What is not commonly known are those mysterious astrological qualities that under girded them, as in the case of the hidden forces of gravity and magnetism. With Neptune, we also get *abstract, the*. However, it is far more than that. Bills (1971) also lists *aesthetics* and *affinities* and *air*. The difference between the *ideas* of Uranus and the *apparitions* of Neptune is how each influences the lives of the masses of people. Environmental poisoning and pollution impacts everyone and is frequently hidden.

Neptune is about *beguiling* and *believing*. It is the whimsical, the scintillation sparkle on the *bubble*, and the flutter of a *butterfly's* experiences that each human being can have. Neptune, the Roman name for the Greek god Poseidon, symbolically has been with us since Homer's Odysseus blinded Poseidon's son Polyphemus the cyclops. Odysseus did this through *deception*, another Neptunian correspondence.

Neptune is *concealment* and *mythology* and was always about emotional expression or watery voyages: *ships, shipping, and shippers*, on bodies of fresh and saltwater. For centuries in the US, Neptune was blatantly manifested as hidden prejudices in the emotional views of *slavery and owning slaves*. It took a civil war to disabuse the people of that practice! But practices die hard, and today's slavery, treating another race as inferior, is practiced more subtly—hidden.

It is disguised in a system that permits the incarceration of disproportionate numbers of people of color and where even greater numbers of people are held down in a corrupt economy, where the majority, including all races, exist near poverty levels. The US also practices a great fog of deception and mendacity surrounding the politics of votes, voting, and voters." Elections have been upheld and practiced for centuries, yet there was still great controversy as recently as the 2016 presidential election.

This author believes that Neptune illuminated is about the "*(unmasking)*" of hidden forces, of Eureka-like experiences and epiphanies. It is Neptune's discovery moment, the revelation of a thing *not on the map* of consciousness. It can also be "*(unrest, widespread)*", and of Utopia, *utopianism.* Finally, Neptune is *visions,* the way through to change and the *visionaries* who see that pathway forward.

For example, when the US Neptune is most active, and there is some significant transit; when the US is at war and masses of people are confused and scared, they seek a new vision. The American Revolution, WWII, and Vietnam are examples of such Neptunian times. The US has been fighting in wars for over 90 percent of its 242-year history. I did my own calculations and will unpack these findings further on in book two.

The epic discovery of Neptune by Gottfried Galle and his assistant, Heinrich d'Arrest, on September 24, 1846, elicited the amazing "not on the map!" statement made by d'Arrest at the time. This famous and exalting exclamation inspired me, and I have chosen to use it as the title of this primer (2017). That planet's revelation, in 1846, synchronized with a buildup of difficult Neptunian themes in the world, including a *sentiment for the abolition of slavery,* which peaked in the US with the outbreak of the American Civil War in April 1861, in Charleston, South Carolina harbor.

Using America's horoscope, it was then technically possible to unveil the *not on the map* astrological realities happening for the US. As it was, the nation was not evolved enough to that point. It was still an adolescent country, barely one Uranus-cycle old (eighty-four years), struggling to find its way in the community of nations. It is this author's hope that the country is now evolved to appreciate, understand, and use this knowledge.

So it was in a season, when all those corresponding Neptune issues surfaced and dominated that the potential for this use was demonstrated. During the last great American season of Neptune on the time of its return in 1938 leading up to and during WWII that certain things Neptune that were likely to happen together came together. This synchronized with the historic planet Returns of Mars and Uranus during the war—a great teaching moment.

The words of Mars, Uranus, and Neptune became common descriptors of WWII, found in daily use, words heard broadcasted on the radio to tens of millions and found printed in the newspapers and periodicals. *I mean words like the army, armaments, bombings, chaos, fear, killing, naval ships, surprise attacks, technological conversions from peacetime manufacturing to military manufacture, and much more. I would add to that notorious words specific to the time like concentration camps and genocide.*

I have mentioned that Neptune's discovery season synchronized with concealed issues being unmasked! The Civil War revealed a serious flaw in American ideals about the equality of human beings. People deceived themselves into thinking that the problem could be ignored indefinitely. This was not to be the case.

The reckoning for that flaw came fourscore and seven years after the creed was set down in the founding Declaration of Independence document. *Not on the map* in the decade prior to the US Civil War, Neptune's emergence as a physical reality and Uranus's first Return hit like a tidal wave to the US psyche. These events synchronized with the crisis, reminiscent of Thomas Paine's *The American Crisis* during the winter of Valley Forge during revolutionary times. Uranus represented explosive, revolutionary, unstable events like the breaking apart of the Union during the Civil War, after certain poisonous Neptune realities were *unmasked as no longer tenable.*

After Uranus mathematically returned to 8° Gemini 55', where it was on July 4, 1776, seven southern states seceded from the Union. Feelings that were long under the surface became concrete actions. This exodus occurred during the Uranus Retrograde Period from 12° Gemini 01' on September 17, 1860, to 7° Gemini 59' on February 14, 1860. South Carolina was the first to declare on December 20, 1860, when Uranus was retrograde at 9° Gemini 15'.

In the next forty-three days, Mississippi, Florida, Alabama, Georgia, and Louisiana, broke from the Union. Texas was the last, declaring on February 1, 1861, before the war broke out. When President Lincoln took his first inaugural oath on March 4, 1861, transiting Uranus was in direct motion at 8° Gemini 05' headed to its final Return at 8° Gemini 55' and completion of America's first full Uranus cycle. The US would not realize another Uranus cycle until 1943, during WWII (1943–45).

Horoscope 4. Planet positions of Mars and Uranus at the start of the American Civil War.

| ♂ | Mars | Gemini | 3rd | 06° Ⅱ 02' |
| ♅ | Uranus | Gemini | 3rd | 09° Ⅱ 21' |

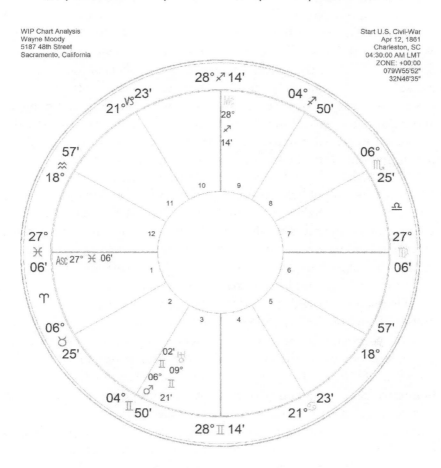

It was the worst-case expression of Uranus for the country—the Uranian breakup materialized as a house violently divided, a people

KEY WIP BRANCHES: 35° NORTH & SOUTH ~ 6° NORTH & SOUTH
10° EAST ~ 103° EAST ~ 77° WEST ~ 169° WEST ~ 3° WEST

ideologically under existential threat. Before the transiting Uranus, in direct motion, exactly contacted the US Uranus position again—backtracking (retrograde) for its second forward-moving Return contact, the breakaway confederacy led by South Carolina fired on Fort Sumter, in Charleston, South Carolina, harbor.

Neptune's long, slow activation in the US horoscope synchronized with an unprecedented history of American war activity nearly two decades, beginning with the Mexican War in 1846 through the Civil War to April 1864. Those eighteen years, between the Mexican-American War and the Civil War, reshaped the beliefs of the American masses who were contesting across the North American continent. These years timed the emergence of innovative war—making technologies and culminated with things like the ironclads on the naval vessels the Monitor and the Merrimack. These weapons of war came into shocking manifestation out of the need to innovate superior weapons.

New beliefs about freedom, music that moved the soul (Battle Hymn of the Republic), inspiring poetry (Walt Whitman's *Leaves of Grass*), the belief-shaking story by Harriet Beecher Stowe (*Uncle Tom's Cabin*), and a myriad of newly applied words, Confederate and Yankee among them descended on America. It was an enveloping zeitgeist reality that subsumes everything—a zeitgeist made up of all those Neptunian things that liked to happen together.

There are many realities and they frequently coexist simultaneously and often in conflict! Astrology's correspondences range widely with a broad spectrum of meanings, representing opposing positions. For example, there was at the same time in America a widespread belief in as well as significant disagreement about slavery. Supposedly reasonable, honorable people were on both sides of the moral disagreement. There was no moral certainty. There were simultaneously expressed visions of a way forward toward change, amid widespread unrest. Utopian dreams of freedom and liberty stood side by side with dystopian ideas of how the structure of American society should look.

In this zeitgeist, a profound Neptunian invention manifested. Photography seemingly came into existence just to photograph all the tumult of the times. Human beings played in this atmosphere with all these new beliefs, developments, glamor, and ways to see themselves reflected, as if with toys. But these were not toys; they were reckonings, lethal reality checks. Future generations would have visual records to remember the lessons of the mid nineteenth century America. The camera was used to photograph the grisly aftermath of Antietam, the costliest battle in American history.

As it happened during the desperate fight for independence in 1776, the distinctive WIP that formed in the US horoscope was a grounded reflection of the *as above* the skyward symbols, grounded in the *so below* on Earth. Born out of those times, Mars, Uranus, and Neptune symbols came to be frozen, fixed in the character and nature of the new country. A warlike expression, written about by historians, continues to this day. In 1861, the chapter heading of that history book was US Civil War!

The symbols representing the lofty ideals set down in the US Declaration of Independence had evolved during four score and seven years leading to the Civil War. Instead of feeling an existential threat from a British invasion by sea, Americans came to fear their fellow Americans; xenophobia reigned across the homeland. The brother was the other!

The impulse for unity and the will to fight the other turned inward compounded by the original flaw in the US design for unity. The nation had a cancer within its body, revealed most brazenly via the institution of slavery. At the time of the Civil War, during the 1860 US Census, there were 3,950,528 million slaves in the US out of a total population of 31,183,582 people. This was 13 percent of the US population at the time. Today, African-American still constitute 13.3 percent of the US population that has grown ten-fold.

Those long-ago words, "That all men are created equal, that they are endowed by their creator with certain unalienable rights" conveyed a standard that was not honored. There was a sense in the air, that future generations were obliged to meet that ideal, that promise, won by the spirited defense during the American Revolution. In the heat of the Civil War, President Lincoln delivered iconic words from an American battlefield, words like none before it.

At Gettysburg, Lincoln spoke of unresolved obligations and tests, rooted in the arguments over issues of slavery, that had destined the nation to unprecedented pain and suffering. It took a costly civil war to start the attempt to settle accounts. Today, that work remains incomplete with evidence of unresolved tensions everywhere, some buried in the earth like unexploded ordnances.

KEY WIP BRANCHES: 35° NORTH & SOUTH ~ 6° NORTH & SOUTH
10° EAST ~ 103° EAST ~ 77° WEST ~ 169° WEST ~ 3° WEST

Chapter 2

Navigating a River of Time

*Only in modern western physics has time become part
of a mathematical framework, which we use with our
conscious mind to describe physical events.*

—von Franz

The use of a number as a communal measuring tool, when used to describe physical events such as timing, gives benefits that when balanced with a sound worldview, opens hidden meaning and qualities to things *not on the map*, greatly deepening and enriching our lives. Astrology uses a mathematical framework that is in part cyclical and symbolic, reflective of nature, not just straight-line linear. In astrology, numbers are joined in a relationship with a symbolic language that describes and mirrors the natural world's expression.

Thus, around 6:30 a.m. each day, at a certain latitude (distance from the equator), the words a dawning sun, daybreak, or a sunrise accurately describe a cherished event. A number representing time acquires profound meaning. In like fashion, numbers representative of a year cycle can be used to track the progress of each new day.

In a 24-hour day or a span of 1440 minutes, a progression of numbers, paired to symbols, assigns meaning that has the potential for great utility. Astrologers have tamed numbers, into degrees and minutes, harnessing them to serve as tools. That utility of numbers is wedded to an astrological scheme, organized under twelve zodiac signs, showing time moving across an east point, the ASCENDANT or sunrise, a point where the Earth and sky reliably meet.

Illustration/Photo 3. Instant of day/night pattern across planet.

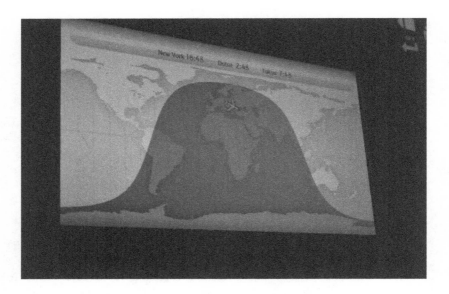

Numbers and signs in the US horoscope are key to unlocking the doorway to the *WIP*. The three planets (Mars, Uranus, and Neptune) making up the *WIP* are each paired with numbers and signs. I have already unpacked the three planets that comprise the *WIP*, but I also want to shed some light on what meanings the two signs, Gemini and Virgo, contribute in the context of war. These signs describe the staging where the three planets manifest.

This is also a good point in the primer for me to share more on the *not on the map* intelligence revealed by astrology signs, symbols, and numbers. As you have seen in the horoscope wheel of the *WIP*, each planet symbol is accompanied by numbers and a sign (i.e., ♂ **at** 21° ♊ 22'). They are also located in one of twelve house divisions of the horoscope.

The *WIP* has two out of the twelve zodiacal signs. The Mars and Uranus parts are in Gemini ♊, while the Neptune component of the *WIP* is in Virgo ♍.

KEY WIP BRANCHES: 35° NORTH & SOUTH ~ 6° NORTH & SOUTH
10° EAST ~ 103° EAST ~ 77° WEST ~ 169° WEST ~ 3° WEST

Horoscope 5. Another look at the distilled US 3-planet WIP.

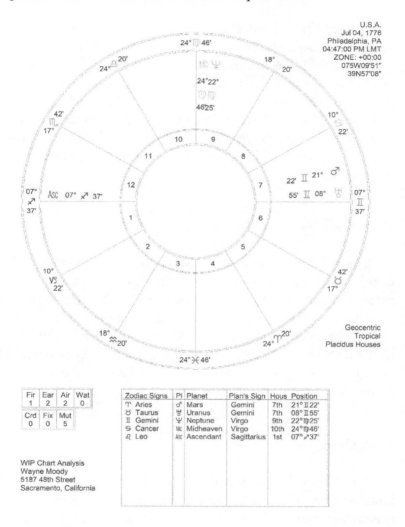

Fir	Ear	Air	Wat
1	2	2	0

Crd	Fix	Mut
0	0	5

WIP Chart Analysis
Wayne Moody
5187 48th Street
Sacramento, California

Zodiac Signs		Pl	Planet	Plan's Sign	Hous	Position
♈	Aries	♂	Mars	Gemini	7th	21°Ⅱ22'
♉	Taurus	♅	Uranus	Gemini	7th	08°Ⅱ55'
Ⅱ	Gemini	♆	Neptune	Virgo	9th	22°♍25'
♋	Cancer	Mc	Midheaven	Virgo	10th	24°♍46'
♌	Leo	Asc	Ascendant	Sagittarius	1st	07°♐37'

Novice 2 Wheel

KEY WIP BRANCHES: 35° NORTH & SOUTH ~ 6° NORTH & SOUTH
10° EAST ~ 103° EAST ~ 77° WEST ~ 169° WEST ~ 3° WEST

In the Gemini ♊ Sign

Gemini, one of three astrological air signs, concerns itself with communicating and traveling through the Earth's atmosphere. Gemini is the realm of ideas, information sharing, and thinking. In the context of warfare, Gemini describes all things linked to American military expression that involves staging of war in the air. Modern language correspondences for Gemini include: air, airplanes, airmail, air traffic controllers, engineers, mechanics, news, and radio. All these come together as, "certain things that like to happen together" in military applications.

With Mars ♂

The US is built upon acting Mars. When you combine Mars with Gemini, Mars at 21° Gemini 22', the signature numerical symbolic expression describes military applications in the twenty-first century that include: cyberwarfare, B-2 stealth bombers, F-35 fighter jets, Hellfire missiles, Predator Drones, and Tomahawk Cruise Missiles. In the wide spectrum of possible meanings, correspondences, Mars in Gemini is the aggressive forward pass in football during the Annual Army-Navy Game.

With Uranus ♅

The United States is built upon radical (Uranus) ideas. The US Uranus, at 8° Gemini 55', manifests in cutting-edge technological systems like the US Aegis Ballistic Missile Defense System, the Patriot Missile Defense System, the Terminal High Altitude Area Defense (THAAD) now being deployed in active branches of the *WIP*. There is an overlap between what Mars brings (war application) and Uranus brings (industrial-scale, technological innovation) that describes this modern technological warfare.

In the Virgo ♍ Sign

Virgo is about making discerning choices. Found early in Rex E. Bills's (1971) alphabetized Virgo listings are terms specifically about armed forces, national health, and the maintenance of the systems designed to support them. What America believes in and chooses to value determines national military goals (defense budgets, size of armed forces, deployments, weapons systems and the like) and the disciplines and other structures necessary to operationalize them.

With Neptune ♆

Join Neptune with the Virgo ♍ sign at 22° 25' and you widen the meaning of the number-matched symbols, to embrace Neptune's correspondence with belief, ideology, and spirit. In the embrace of this US Neptunian reality are held the American ideals about liberty, as well as the inspired American Yankee patriot, both iconized at the center of US military history. Neptune's connection to the collective, the masses, makes sense of America's history of citizen soldier, its eras of compulsory conscription, draft armies, and militias. Now its memes on social median driving public opinion and fake news.

Neptune's links with compassion and sacrifice are readily experienced in the national, highly promoted, American Memorial Day (happening with sun in Gemini on the last Monday in May) and Veterans' Day observances. The decades long promotion of the glamor of smoking and drinking in the military, with the liberal distribution of alcohol and cigarette rations, is an outdated Neptunian expression. It gave way to massive drug addiction among soldiers during the Vietnam War. You see, even the understanding of the symbol of Neptune in Virgo slowly changed over the centuries.

Neptune is synonymous with chemical gases, with issues to do with the nervous system, and with all manner of poisons. In 2000, US chemical weapons stores were transported thousands of miles from military storage areas, from bases around the Earth, and destroyed at Johnston Island, at the Johnston Atoll Chemical Agent Disposal System in the dawn of the twenty-first century. The current official US policy on the use of chemical weapons in war is that it is a war crime.

Johnston Island, located at 169° West 31'26", is in the heart of the Neptune ASC and Mars MH branches of the *WIP* running through the Pacific Ocean.

Reading the Numbers

Numbers bring their own special component to the *WIP* reality. Besides their great use in mathematics and physics, they have their own, *not on the map*, symbolic component, which when considering them, opens a door to tremendous insights. We have three numbers to unpack here: the 21 associated with Mars, the 8 with Uranus, and 22 with Neptune.

Horoscope Data 7. The three WIP planets with numbers.

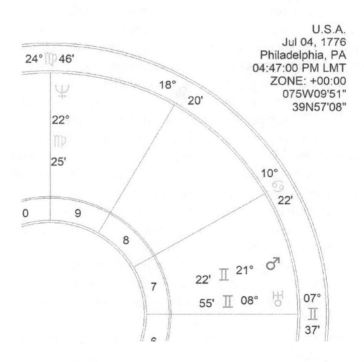

Some special astrological applications of these numbers require that they be rounded to the next highest number. For example, the US Mars is at 21° Gemini 22", which rounds to number 22°. The specificity of these numbers is key to various wisdom systems, ranging from the astrological and numerological to the placements of Fixed Stars, and what are known in the astrological community as Sabian Symbols.

21° GEMINI 22'

Looked at through yet another lens, Numerology master Annemarie Schimmel writes in *The Mystery of Numbers* that the number 21 is considered the number of perfection, the product of two sacred numbers 3 and 7. The US Mars placement is 21° Gemini 22", rounded to 22°, which produces a number key in the Kabbalah or Tree of Life, which has 22 symbolic pathways. The tarot is an oracle that has been used since the 16th century.

"It consists of a pack of 78 cards which are divided into two main groups: one group of 22 cards, the major arcana" (Banzhaf, 2000). The symbolism of these 22 cards tells an archetypal story of the human journey through life. For example, there is one called the Fool. Of the 22 cards, all but the Fool are numbered.

This card symbolizes a hero who makes a great journey. Full of naivete and trust, he is also clever, courageous, strong, and unwavering. This symbolism is universal, found in the heroes of many different cultures. The American soldier is idealized in this way.

Another source of wisdom comes from the Fixed Stars. Fixed Stars are those bodies in the celestial sky that do not appear to move during an average human lifetime. They do move, just extremely slowly.

These fixed stars make up our constellations, those easily recognized patterns like Orion, made up of major fixed stars like Bellatrix. The stars of Orion have great relevance to the WIP Mars. Fixed Star-wise, there are two Fixed Stars at 21° Gemini, both are on the US Mars. This is *not on the map* knowledge. You have to know some things. They are Bellatrix an Unfortunate Star and Capella, a Fortunate Star. Bellatrix is Orion's left shoulder and is connected to sudden dishonor. Capella, also at 22° Gemini, militarily has opportunities for powerful friends.

The Orion Nebula is on the sword at Orion's waist. Mars corresponds to sword. (Bills, 1971) The US WIP is locked at the hip to the myth of Orion and his warlike nature, a gift which had consequences for him.

Rounding the US Mars (21° Gemini 22') to 22° Gemini gives three Fortunate Fixed Star hits: to Phat, showing talent in science; Mintaka, the possibility of a high position; and El Nath, connected with weapons of war – again a sword – and point of attack. In another astrological system, the modern Sabian Symbol System (1925), 21°–22° Gemini is visualized as "Dancing Couples in A Harvest Festival."

8° Gemini 55'

Numerology master Schimmel writes that the number 8 is an auspicious number, whereas 9 becomes "the magnified sacred 3." There is the Fixed Star, Aldebaran, considered an Unfortunate Star at 9° Gemini 47' (today), in the reach of the US Uranus 8° Gemini 55' placement. Aldebaran is one of four ancient Royal Stars. Its meanings include, Watcher of the East and Warmonger. Considered Fortunate by some, but any honors carry immense risk and responsibility.

The astrological Sabian Symbol System describes 9° Gemini as "A Quiver Filled with Arrows." This is remarkable intelligence for the military to be conscious of given that it is describing Uranus in the *WIP*. I can't help but think of America's WWII reputation as the "Arsenal of Democracy." This is intelligence that goes to congenitally set character patterns for the US.

22° Virgo 25'

Numerology master Schimmel records that the number 22 produces a number key to understanding the Sephiroticum System and the 22 mystery pictures of the Tarot. The rounded number 23, has no hidden meaning in Schimmel's book. However, the US Neptune is bracketed by two Fixed Stars, one Unfortunate and the other Fortunate.

Denebola at 21° Virgo 46' (today) is Unfortunate, possibly bringing criticism, perseverance, honors, undesirable associates to military affairs, to name a few outcomes. The second bracket is Coma Berenices, a Fortunate Star at 23° Virgo 56' (today) bringing eye problems, a suave manner, with great personal charm to the US military experience. This describes quite a few great American military commanders. Franklin Delano Roosevelt, America's 32nd US President and Commander-In-Chief during WWII, had an AA-Rodden Rated horoscope with 23° Virgo 16' on his critical Ascendant Angle. Famous US military leaders, like Generals George Patton (his North Node ☊), Norman Schwarzkopf (his Progressed Ascendant on January 17, 1991-Desert Storm) or James Mattis (his Saturn ♄), often had/have meaningful, strong, tight and straightforward astrological aspects between their birth horoscope placements and the US horoscope placements. They made or are making US military history.

The astrological Sabian Symbol for the US Neptune placement (22° + rounded to 23° Virgo) is "A Lion Tamer Displays His Skill and Character." It takes art, craft, method, patience, recognition, skill, and wisdom, to blend the information just presented into a reading that matches the reality of an FDR in time of war. As was just mentioned and bares repeating, his horoscope, with its AA-Rodden Rating, had 23° Virgo 16' on the most important and sensitive angle of the horoscope - the Ascendant.

House Numbers

The planet placement in the horoscope wheel and the house numbers, also carry information. These house numbers highlight staging. What will be the contextual look of identity, of possessions, familiarity, or sense of home for the planet? Mars and Uranus both occupy the horoscope's 7th House. At its core, this is the stage describing your relationship to the other. What world of objects and people bring you to balance? Importantly, in context with the *WIP*, the 7th House is called the House of *open enemies*. Japanese Zero fighter aircraft bombed Pearl Harbor. Ultimately air power decided the war in the Pacific from Midway to Hiroshima.

Horoscope Data 8. US – 7ᵗʰ House planets.

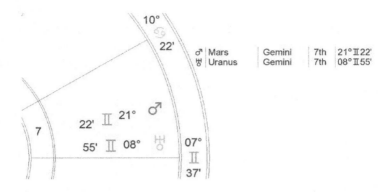

Neptune is in the horoscope's 9ᵗʰ house. This house is largely about how the staging for the county's growth looks to the public; its manifestations have to do with American higher education, geographic growth, knowledge base, and philosophical orientation. *I'm talking about the core beliefs, ideals, and stories of the American journey.*

Horoscope Data 9. Neptune on US midheaven (MH) angle.

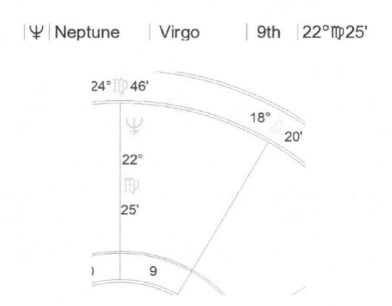

My purpose here is to help you realize a not on the map philosophical orientation and the different forms that it can take. With these numbers and sign helpers, the planets can be better appreciated and organized to reveal their *not on the map* secrets.

It is gratifying and truly amazing when, after long study and careful research, the symbolism of any horoscope reveals itself to an astrologer's eye. General Norman Schwarzkopf did not have obvious connections in his AA-Rodden Rated horoscope to the WIP numbers. But there was one startling synchronicity in his horoscope aligned with the US WIP Neptune, when he commanded Operation Desert Storm. Only after using a secondary progression tool to move his horoscope forward in time to January 17, 1991, the year he commanded Desert Storm, do we establish a strong link. Schwartzkopf's progressed Ascendant was at 23° Virgo 41'.

Coming to WIP conscious was hard won. Finding it and mastering the cartography has been a life's work. Putting what has been revealed, before the public, in a responsible way is my next step. The skillful application of this previously *not on the map* intelligence in the world, of what has been rendered as a tool of insight, has become my purpose.

I cannot repeat this too often. My purpose in writing this book, revealing what was previously unknown, is to help make clearer lines of understanding between countries that may come into conflict with other nations on this finite Earth. A threat to a country's interests (food, energy, resources for industry, security, and water) does not need to automatically lead to war.

My hope is that when the nations of the world better understand and appreciate each other's needs, there will be a greater willingness to make accommodations. Knowing the specific where, when, who, and what fault lines exist between countries can help focus any negotiations to the core issues. The US *WIP* example gives more information to supplement existing knowledge and provides leaders with more options for resolving conflict(s) between countries. Look no further than China and the South China Sea, or Turkey and it's southerneastern border with Syria, specifically Northeastern Syria.

Additionally, juxtaposed with the US *WIP* is an American horoscope Pluto line, tracing along 50° East longitude through the Arabian/Persian Gulf. This line has been and still is existentially important to the US economy and its industry. We must be aware of the existence and locations of the four angular US Pluto lines after 2019, as Pluto transits closer to its epic Return, in the US horoscope, exact in February 2022. Another US Pluto line sweeps near Beijing, China. *Problems need to be addressed now, immediately; we are a little more than 2 years out. Time is precious!* Time is running out! *Dear reader, it is critically important in this twenty-first century global world that you learn your geography and history!*

Chapter 3

Horoscope Symbols and the Twelve Signs of the Zodiac

The twelve houses of the horoscope are synonymous with the twelve signs of the Zodiac, commonly recognizable by many when they look into the night sky. In a person's horoscope, they are briefly in order: Aries—willpower, Taurus—sensual, Gemini—mental type, Cancer—empathic type, Leo—center of power, Virgo—a critical point of view, Libra—the sense of balance, beauty and proportion, Scorpio—extreme situations, Sagittarius—soaring consciousness, Capricorn—sense of purpose, Aquarius—universal spirit, and Pisces—tremendous sensitivity.

In modern usage, Mars is the planet ruler assigned Aries. The first horoscope House division collectively shares themes of assertiveness, acting straightforward, showing parts of one's nature, being courageous, and taking risks. These are some of the correspondences in a person's horoscope. Mundanely (astrology of nations), Aries, Mars, and the first house are about a country's people. The *WIP* features Mars.

The following are some qualities suggested by the signs in a country's horoscope, they are in order: Aries—willpower of the people, Taurus—sensual qualities of the culture, Gemini—a nation's ideas, Cancer—emotional temperament of the people, Leo—centers of attention, Virgo—a people's collective critical point of view, Libra—the cultural aesthetic, Scorpio—extreme situations, Sagittarius—foreign relations—open enemies, Capricorn—leadership structures, Aquarius—humanitarian impulses, spirit, and Pisces—compassion, humanity, sense of unity.

In *Mundane Astrology: The Astrology of Nations and States* (Raphael, Carter, Green, 2004), Raphael lists: "soldiers, surgeons, noted military and naval men, war, disputes, fire, and incendiarism," as some Mars expressions. This book focuses upon the military expression of the WIP planets which include Mars. The 1st house—Mars ruled—correspondences given by Raphael's are "the common people, public health, general conditions of the country, and state of home affairs generally." On the other hand, the traditional Libra, 7th House symbolism, ruled by Venus, has the opposite concerns, focusing upon balancing oneself in the world of others, being passive, or receptive as the object of Arian assertiveness—the power of an attractive force to a projecting force. Raphael's gives the 7th House correspondence with "foreign affairs, and relations with other powers, War [*sic*] and international disputes, Marriages, [*sic*] divorces, foreign trade."

Few are born with a horoscope with 0 degrees of Aries, appearing on the first house angle. One would have to be born exactly where and when the Vernal Equinox clocked in. In reality, twelve different signs can mark that all-important first house, also called the ASCENDANT ASC Angle. These twelve possibilities are greatly embellished by the relationship patterns—the planet aspects that are present in the horoscope circle.

All horoscope planets pay homage to the ASC degree and sign. It has no equal in importance. This is why a Rodden Rating (RR) is so important to this *WIP* study. It is on and through that ASC/1st-house stage, where the planet performs. So whichever of the twelve signs marks this most sensitive point in any horoscope, there is a method for measuring each planet's temperament and availability, expressing through the ASC. Knowing the spectrum of correspondences choices for the planets in the signs helps one gain access to the *not on the map* knowledge behind the symbols.

In summary, *a horoscope begins with the first house, marked with one of twelve signs, beginning what is known as the symbolically supreme ASCENDANT ASC ANGLE.* This ASC is considered the body or face of the horoscope. If it is the horoscope of a common person, or *People* in the case of a country's horoscope, it goes far in symbolically describing physical appearance, character and development. Here is the US ASC—degree and sign—used to establish the *WIP planets aligned to* two angles.

Horoscope Data 10. US ASCENDANT ASC ANGLE.

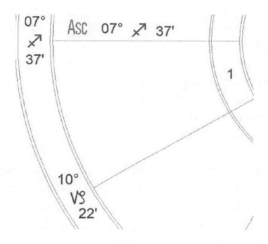

| Asc | Ascendant | Sagittarius | 1st | 07°⚏37' |

The ASC number and symbolism go to the expression, form and health of a person's body. If the horoscope is that of an entity, the ASC describes the outward impressions, inclinations, the superficially perceived affect of that entity (bank, corporation, country, kingdom, or nation) in the world.

The ASCENDANT and 1ˢᵗ house of any horoscope corresponds with manifestation, its appearance, and form. It is a symbol for all of the body's actions, style of movement, strength, and ultimate physical health. Ruled by Mars, it is about life, about robust vitality, and these are the qualities one wants in a soldier, hence Mars god of war!

In Homer's *Odyssey*, Mars is Hector's power, indeed the power of the Trojan army, whose sponsor was *bloody* Ares, the Greek god who favored the Trojans, during the Trojan War, aligning against the other gods. Athena the goddess of war, supported the Greek side in the war.

The flag of a country is a symbol for its ASC and becomes its pride. In the American flag, red, the majority color, is a true correspondent to Mars. The ubiquitous red in American culture hints at the not on the map equally all-pervasive Mars in the American character.

The Mars expression in the *War Impulse Pattern (WIP)* is considerable. From the time of Ptolemy, 100 AD, over 2,000 years ago, red has been associated with Mars. Dr. Lee Lehman documents this in her book *The Book of Rulerships: Keywords from Classical Astrology* (Lehman, 1993). Ptolemy also saw Mars as *bloodthirsty*. Continental Congress Secretary Charles Thompson on June 20, 1782, noted that red symbolizes hardiness and valor, but, dear reader, we know it can also easily be associated with the blood of the fallen in war. Mars has been attributed to blood as far back as the great Arab astrologer al-Biruni during Crusader times. Mars gives the warfare nature to the *WIP* name. Since Mars is part of a three-part pattern, it must contend with the awesome forces of the outer planets Uranus and Neptune, realities not subject to human will. To fight and win, Americans need to believe in causes!

In this formidable team, Mars is compromised, directed, and subsumed by greater symbolic forces. If Mars is to realize any of its more reasonable qualities—courage, persistence and strength it must master discipline in teamwork. Mars is exalted in the Capricorn sign and 10th house, both of which favor discipline.The US Mars is well expressed in American popular culture through sports and activities involving technological advances. Think NASCAR racing. When poorly deployed, Mars's expression in the US is mass impulsiveness and recklessness, made difficult because of the *outer planet* nature of Uranus and Neptune in the trio. Think *Animal House* fraternities. Think Japanese Internment—Executive Order 9066.

Astrologically viewed, the *outer planets* are said to drown out and overwhelm p*ersonal planet* expression. Uranus shares the same Gemini sign as Mars in the US horoscope, which is linked in what is called a 90-degree square □ aspect to Neptune's degree. The square aspect is a measure of stress between two positions. Uranus joins Mars in the consequences of managing this stress, within the *WIP*.

When you read a horoscope, you are making use of the fact that the planets making up the horoscope continue to change positions in the actual zodiacal sky or move through the map of reality that is the horoscope. The ability to measure planet movements is a formidable tool in the astrologer's toolbox. The horoscope calculated at birth is sacred and specific to the individual—it is a benchmark. It is a moment frozen in time! A horoscope fixes the planet positions like push plates, against which future comparisons can be made. Whatever is unique in one's horoscope stands as a measure of character of uniqueness for life! *Recall the list of US presidents who were born intimately tied to the WIP planets. Remember too there are other important players like US ambassador to Iraq April Glaspie, who were seemingly scripted to play critical roles on active branches of the WIP.*

Recalling the aspects, those certain numerically measured relationships that give articulation to the expression of a horoscope. When the Sun makes its Return each year, a 360° cycle is completed, a birth year is celebrated. The clock resets to 0°, beginning a new cycle. In American culture, the birthday or Solar Return (SR) is an event celebrated by most people.

Even the nation's birthday, the Fourth of July, is celebrated and was celebrated by its principal architects John Adams and Thomas Jefferson during their lifetimes. Both Adams (aged ninety) and Jefferson (aged eighty-two) died on the 50th Fourth of July anniversary in 1826. It could be said that their passing timed the passing of their generation's influence and management of the US.

This annual Solar Return (SR) to 13° Cancer 18' in the national horoscope is called a conjunction ♂ aspect (0°) by astrologers. Conjunctions occur, when a celestial body transiting the zodiac makes a complete circuit of the 360-degree horoscope wheel and exactly Returns to its original horoscope position. In actual practice, if a body is close, within a certain predetermined orb of sensitivity up to 15 degrees in some cases concerning the Sun, it is in conjunction.

After one's birthday, the completed year begins anew with the Sun energized, striving forward in the zodiac to begin a new season of travel through the horoscope, conjuncting in turn each of the different planet parts. This allows for the re-energizing of each component of the horoscope by turns. It applies to all the different planets, determined by their different orbits around the Sun.

Mercury takes but 88 days to transit a horoscope, Mars—2 years, Jupiter—12 years, while Uranus takes 84 years and Neptune, 161 years. Pluto, totally off the map of individual reality, takes an eye-popping

248 years to orbit the Sun. You can see that a citizen would have but one Uranus Return in a normal human lifespan, but a country can have many Uranus Returns. The US will have its third Uranus Return on July 27, 2027. Each of the Uranus Returns have synchronized war. This is good intelligence.

Astrological aspects take the measure of a 360-degree circle. Aspect meanings, such as, for the conjunction, are *challenge, intensity* and *to unite,* provide the necessary vocabulary to construct a narrative. Intense events are synchronized when the two WIP outer planets, including Mars's Return by association. Any Return to an original position is an aspect of 0° degrees. Returns synchronize with significant renewals and endings. When the Sun has progressed one quarter of the circle, or the year cycle, it has traveled for 90 days or for 90° degrees of that circle. This quartering of a year is the equivalent of spring equinox, summer solstice, fall equinox, and winter solstice divisions. Events mark radical changes. Rhink winter to spring, summer to autumn.

A country's horoscope, measured in this way by the Sun's seasonal movement, gives similar useful information. The seasonal change to spring, when the transiting Sun crosses into the ASC house of any nation can be a spring-like time of significant renewal. Because the US has a Sagittarius ASC, this happens for the US each year on the fourth Thursday of November, as the transiting Sun, moving through the zodiac, nears 7° degrees of Sagittarius. This happens around the time when America celebrates its annual, since 1863, Thanksgiving holiday. The astrological Sagittarius corresponds with foreign lands, anything big—huge meals, immigrants, long journeys home, great spiritual undertakings. Why Thursday? Well, for one, the US came into existence on a Thursday.

There are other aspects to consider, primary to the dramatic conjunction ♂ Returns are movements of slow moving planets across the angles of the horoscope. While Uranus and Neptune are very slow moving through a horoscope, there are time frames that present momentous developments and are useful in a human or the nation's lifetime. When Uranus has completed half of its cycle, age forty-two years for most people, there dawns a period of life that astrologers call the Mid Life Crisis. Neptune will have moved 90 degrees to its original position. Half of the Neptune cycle finds people in their eighties, deep (in the modern era) into their retirement. They are considered Elders in some cultures, rich in experience, even acknowledged, as *National Treasures i*n some societies for what they bring. Think Japan. The average American lifespan does not reach age eighty.

For you younger readers, here's some information you might find interesting and helpful. Gail Sheehy wrote a book (1976) titled *Passages*. What is *not on the map* is awareness that the book dealt with the same measures of time, Saturn, Neptune, Uranus, and Pluto cycles (without mentioning them) that astrologers use to measure times of major crises in most human lives. She specifically referred to the seven-year itch ages seven, fourteen, twenty-one, and twenty-eight years of age.

Astrologers call age twenty-eight, the Saturn Return—a major astrological event! Think Shakepeare's pastoral comedy As You Like It, "All the World's a Stage", his seven seasons of life. It is said that Sheehy's book was meant to locate the personality changes common to each stage of life. She compared the developmental rhythms of men and women—which she found strikingly unsynchronized and considering this, to examine the crises that couples can anticipate. Which passages cause one partner to put an extra strain on the other? How do their needs and dreams change with age?

The square between Mars (personal planet) and Neptune (outer planet) can represent motivation, pressure, collective pressure, or the zeitgeist, being pushed by collective engagement and action. This is not necessarily a good or a bad thing. It could be simply chalked up to context. When is conflict, effort, pressure, or pushing happening and sometimes necessary? I grew up Black during the height of the Civil Rights struggle. At times I and my siblings, resembled cannon fodder, desegregating American public schools, colleges and institutions. Think Ruby Bridges. Think Authur Ash.

Another example, when one is born during a depression or a war— both huge collective events—these events, beyond our individual control, end up the backdrop to our lives. We all live out our individual lives dealing with some such context—loved ones off to war, rationing, blackouts, and martial law. Some of us flow more easily in an age, a Zeitgeist like this, than others. In 1939, there were approximately 2.2 billion people in the world. At the end of WWII that number had grown to 2.3 billion, despite 50–60 million war-related deaths.

In a human horoscope, a near-exact Mars/Neptune square could indicate a person chronically challenged, notably in certain areas of their physical expression, exhibiting a tendency to have conflict in their relationships, difficulty showing courage and taking risks, disbelief, problems acting upon inspiration, or struggles to get work accomplished. Think soldier. It could be the horoscope of a person dying in war. It is Neptune's involvement that frustrates action and adds confusion and weakness. The US horoscope Mars/Neptune-square People could show a tendency to act blindly and appear confused and disoriented in terms of action, show fogginess of their action, or be inspired by a collective vision, good or bad. Think Jonestown, Guyana 1978.

The horoscopes of the first killed, the heroes and leaders during US wars, oftentimes show close, if not exact horoscope ties, to the numbered positions of the US *WIP* planets. My research found many. In their individual stories, there may be issues of belief and faith in one's power or a systemic body weakness. Because it's Neptune involved, for an *outer planet,* the challenges are large shapers in one's life and don't go away. More on outer planets in a bit.

Horoscope Data 11. Mars-square-Neptune pattern in US horoscope.

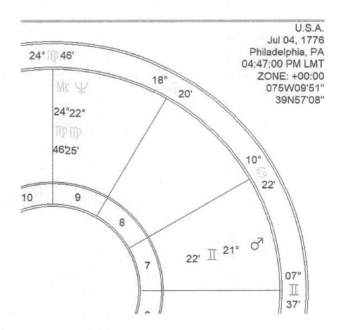

KEY WIP BRANCHES: 35° NORTH & SOUTH ~ 6° NORTH & SOUTH
10° EAST ~ 103° EAST ~ 77° WEST ~ 169° WEST ~ 3° WEST

When the horoscope with the Mars square to Neptune pattern is that of an entity like the US is then even greater concerns present. This is the case with the Mars/Neptune-square pattern in the US horoscope. In a national horoscope the behavior is a collective one and involves periodic bouts of many people acting. Think 49er Gold Rush. Or badly, it is delusional group action. Think Train of Tears out of North Carolina along 35° North. Race riots also come to mind.

The pattern speaks to any struggle within a collective to embrace a unifying set of beliefs represented by the Neptune symbol in the horoscope. It often speaks to a group's ability to rally to a cause. Think Earth Day and Marches against the Vietnam War. This radical rallying is symbolized by Mars in the relationship. It's *Fight the Power*!

Neptune's position, at the highest, most aspirational point of the US horoscope, represents the higher consciousness, learning, and the wisdom of a nation's people. It holds the place of collective beliefs and ideals, philosophy, and wisdom in the 9th house. Getting people to embrace a belief, or take up a cause, is necessary to effect change and spur successful unified action. Think Climate Change. Having people act from their highest ideals is the challenge in the US horoscope. They can play direct roles, when their horoscopes plug tightly into the WIP planets.

Some historical examples:

- The Revolutionary era, George Washington and Nathaniel Green;
- the Civil War era, Robert E. Lee and Nathan Forrest; the Spanish-American War;
- Millennial change brought Theodore Roosevelt to prominence;
- World Wars I and II saw the emergence of Black Jack Pershing, Patton, Eisenhower, Nimitz, Marshall, and Bradley;
- Presidents George H. W. Bush and his son George W. Bush have added whole chapters to America's military changes to the world;
- In 2018, we see the likes of Kelly, Mattis, and the current president all make the list. They are already writing the pages that will add to US military history.

This credential is important in the waging of war. The attention merchants in the American system—the commercial press—the free press—must do the work of educating, informing, and recruiting the public! America's war experiences hold many concrete examples of this. If they are unsuccessful, think Fake News. America's Vietnam experience is a stark lesson in this.

Uranus is the innovative, the unknown surprise element, the X-factor in the *WIP*-trio pattern. Who knew the US would have people in Nevada, USA, and Niamey, Niger, Africa, sitting at computer consoles directing military drone kinetic operations thousands of miles away? And they're situated in the WIP. Who knew? This is exactly the kind of X-Game mindset one needs to imagine future WIP realities. The thinking must always remain out-of-the-box, cutting-edge, original. Uranus in Gemini corresponds with original (Uranus) thinking (Gemini) and for breakups (Uranus) with failed approaches and ideas (Gemini), discarding tools that are outdated, don't work, leading to breakthroughs into new approaches, methods, and tools that do. This process can lead to breakthrough innovations. Think IED.

It can lead to rebellion! Think Anbar uprising in Iraq, the seed of Islamic State (ISIL). Compromises between the hard positions of Mars, Uranus, and Neptune expressions must be made, if the core American ideals, represented by Neptune, at the top of the American horoscope, are necessary to make that strong convincing argument, swaying the minds of the collective US human resources into action.

The trio of planets must work together if any of their best individual qualities are to be met. Author Tim Wu in his book *The Attention Merchants* (Knopf, 2016) writes about the art of propaganda and the great importance placed on capturing people's hearts and minds. In war and in business, propaganda frequently shapes the outcomes. If said another way, in the King James version of the Bible in Proverbs 29:18, "Where there is no vision, the people perish!"

Uranus and Neptune, as *outer planets*, operate on very different levels from that of the *personal* will of Mars. They are considered *outer planets* because of their *out-of-this-world*, long cycle, *way-out-of-the-norm* expression. These otherworldly planets are descriptive of the actions of people acting in collectives, of the synergy experiences of large groups, rather than individuals. Things like 1000-year flood events, major natural disasters and wars are collective events best addressed and survived by group responses. Famously, Cicero objected to astrology, asking did all those who died at the catastrophic of Battle of Cannae, where Hannibal's smaller force defeated a larger Roman force leaving 55,000 dead, share the same horoscope? Think concentration camps. Not everybody experiences these calamities in an 80-year-long-life. Uranus and Neptune are not subject to a person's willpower or even the discipline represented by Saturn (representing nature's laws).

Before Uranus was discovered, it was believed that Saturn was the limiting planet in Earth's Solar System. Recall Galileo and the tremendous challenge he brought to the Catholic world view of reality of a fixed heaven with his book *Dialogue Concerning the Two Chief World Systems* (1632). With his argument championing Copernicus's astronomical discoveries, Galileo shattered the church's propaganda to the masses that the heavens were a fixed system that revolved around a stationary Earth. Galileo is said to have been the first to see Neptune through his telescope in 1613, and he is believed to have known that it moved (like a planet around the sun), but he dismissed its importance. The planet had to remain *not on the map* of human awareness for another 233 years until Galle and d'Arrest rediscovered it in 1846.

A century and three-quarters later, with the discovery of Uranus, the physical limits of a Saturnine to Earth's solar system was intellectually pushed outward, reflecting and synchronizing with a radical expansion in human consciousness development. When the discoveries of Uranus and Neptune came, they synchronized with a widespread growth in collective consciousness. Entire cultures were being changed because of their evolving understanding of the world.

The zeitgeist surrounding Uranus and Neptune discoveries were saturated with poignant events relevant to the naming and articulation of the new realities. Ben Franklin was experimenting with electricity in the season surrounding the 1781 discovery of Uranus. In 1846 there was tremendous cultural activity—encyclopedias, different Enlightenments, human rights movements, and many other unprecedented historical events that synchronized with and later defined the discoveries of the blended planet expressions. Think repeating rifles.

During the times of these awesome planetary discoveries, Freemasons, astrologers did their work and made many connections for the culture. This synchronistic Earth-sky equivalence is a simple idea. Equivalence or correspondence philosophy was thrown into disrepute by the philosophies of reasoning emerging with the scientific age. At the core of this primer on the US *War Impulse Pattern*, is the recognition that correspondence relationships are facts and synchronicities exist.

When you construct a narrative around events like the Declaration of Independence, you deepen and extend their power, readability and actionability through adding astrological correspondence language. Furthermore, the quantitative measure of the horoscope planets allows their orbit times to be used as a timing tool. You can make uncanny forecasts. The resulting blend of symbolic language and time measure permits noncausal relationships, happening between the sky and events on the Earth, to be revealed and more fully appreciated.

Astrologers, early on, embraced Uranus as corresponding with the principles of discoveries, inventions, and revolutions. Things like electricity, free speech, and America came to be associated with the planet. Indeed and importantly, Uranus is emphasized through being angular, on the 7th—angular-house cusp in the US horoscope with the C-Rodden Rating used here.

There are four angles to any horoscope. The ASCENDANT (ASC), or angle rising like the Sun in the east, is the most important, followed by the MIDHEAVEN (top of the horoscope—noon, MC or MH), DESCENDANT (setting—sunset) DSC, and NADIR (midnight) IC. The US Uranus closely aligns with the all-important DESCENDANT angle of the US horoscope.

In a mundate chart, this DSC is largely experienced as the outside world, outside of the US, as foreigners, immigrants.and threatening people—open enemies. Think of US policy and press towards China, Iran and Russia today. The USA is a nation of immigrants, and most people living on American soil today look abroad for their bloodline roots (O'Connor, Lubin, and Spector, 2013). There has always been a huge charge in the US over issues involving immigrants. When there is domestic conflict brewing in America, especially the economic struggles, the stage is simultaneously scripted and set with the emergence of old conditioning, that fear of an invasion of the *New Albion* from the old world, manifesting as immigration issues.

After that defining American 1776 moment, as is the case with all things born, a period of growth and maturation ensued. The country's natural destiny was to mature, to develop itself through many experiences, often painful ones, involving international adversaries and partners. Mundanely, Uranus corresponds with foreign governments that are friends and to as wide a reach into the unusual aspects of the world, as possible, to get the most original and unique exposures. One of America's four A*C*G Uranus lines runs through New Zealand. Think kiwi fruit.

Uranus was the ancient Greek sky god (rainmaker), fertilizing the Earth with its ideals. The beginnings of any nation's horoscope is much like an infant at the beginning of its maturation to adulthood, with the goal being an eventual mastery of some material ideal, a national body, collective emotional, knowledge, and spiritual identity. The extended body of a nation is seen in its commonly held bloodlines to other lands around the Earth, literally the entire Earth! Think African-American, German-American, Irish-American, Italian-American, Mexican-American, and Japanese-American to barely skim the list The mapping component of astrology acknowledges this.

People put parts of their bodies into focus when they work to develop and master fitness through exercise. Since childhood I have been fascinated with my arms and hands. Astrology's correspondence language opens the door to one plausible reason. I was born a Sunsign Gemini, which corresponds with the arms and hands of the anatomy. Nations grow and work their ideal bodies too. America's body at maturity is one that emphasizes and flaunts its Mars internationally. Think US military bases in Germany, Italy and now Niger and Norway, all under the US Mars Ic line.

In the last century, the US has exercised itself internationally leaving a legacy of two bloody wars in Europe and three more, half a world away in Japan, Korea, and Southeast Asian, on Cambodian, Laoian, and Vietnamese battlefields. Major WIP arteries of the US, reflecting geopolitical and astrological realities, reach into regions like Panama and Venezuela, through China. Think iPhone City. For decades now the US national interest has focused along 35° North latitude, through the heartlands of Middle Eastern nations and South Asian lands. Think Axis of Evil. In a fairly shared world, all nations have rights and deserve opportunities to balance their unique cultural formulae, their special requirements, between their neighbors. Think rights like, Life, Liberty and the Pursuit of Happiness.

Cause-and-effect philosophers are limited to seeing reality expressed through linear connections (causes) of physical events between objects

(Newtonian laws). Certain things, that do not obey these cause-and-effect laws, are just *not on the map* for them. Realities like correspondence, synchronistic and like-minded are alien. Their realities simply do not exist; they are invisible to the uninitiated!

Just articulating the causal connections between the American Revolution, like the "shot heard round the world" fired at Lexington and Concord, does not fully illuminate the not on the map meanings and deeply spiritual message of those awesome moments. What was resonating in the capitals of Europe at that time. Not a simple idea, but a Uranian one of Life, Liberty and the Pursuit of Happiness, long before the words were spoken. The events were without precedent in colonial history. It was a time of unforeseen, apparent chance occurrences of rare possibilities in time and place, synchronizing historic breakdowns and outbreaks of violent overthrow of established power. The US *WIP* tool goes far in seeing the memes that took hold in the past and were *not on the map* of the times. Think guillotine.

The message the Uranus discovery delivered to old-established nations was one of enlightenment and freedom. It presented to established structures as rebellion, of the breakdown of control and order, being a reality—of such a possibility as freedom manifesting in their own lands. These were pure Uranus expressions! The horoscope of the Declaration of Independence seen through its twentieth-century-mapping component reveal that a Uranus line traces through the stages of all the major events leading to the rebellion, to places like Boston, Concord, Lexington, New York City, as well as London, England.

Astrology, with its *open-sesame* door to different realities through anachronistic correspondence language and its complete acceptance of synchronicity, argues a philosophy of ancient, deep, much-observed connections. It points to realms of knowing that are, metaphysically deep, below in the cellars of cause-and-effect philosophy. Today, using the astrology lens, any activation of the US Uranus symbolism synchronizing certain specific types of expression in the physical world, can be pinpointed geographically on Uranus-marked map stages. Think Cape Canaveral launches. Cape Canaveral is exactly under the US Uranus Descendant line.

It is worth repeating, that Boston, Lexington, and Concord are all marked by an A*C*G, WIP Uranus influence, running the entire New England Atlantic Coastline and are revealed only in a map generated by US *horoscope.* These historic stages are ever in the grip of the *WIP* climate! A Uranus climate means conditions of constant breakthrough events, running the spectrum, from innovations, Nor'easterners, unprecedented firsts like the Pilgrim's Rock landings, its impact on the indiginous people. It is forethought (Uranus rules astrologers), innovations, and Promethean action. Prometheus is the rebellious Greek titan demigod known for having served humans by revealing the power of fire reserved for gods. From the perspective of this book, New England and Atlantic Coast states brought us the classic arms innovators Colt and Remington. Think gun control and Sandy Hook Shootings.

Reading the US through its horoscope and maps is a Uranian, radically different approach to thinking! Synchronizing a time of radical new ways of thinking, Uranus was first seen and named on March 13, 1781, during what was called the Age of Reason or the Enlightenment (1685–1815). It is ironic that Herschel, the British scientist who discovered the planet, first wanted to name the planet for the American colonials' nemesis King George III of the status quo. George III was the oppressor, named often in the lines of the Declaration of Independence. King George's horoscope has an A- Rodden Rating. His horoscope Sun was 13° Gemini 20', in the midst of the US Mars–21° Gemini 22'–Uranus 8° Gemini 55'.

King George was the catalyst, the object of the rebellion. For many colonists he embodied the real and symbolic arch villain who ordered the British/Hessian invasion of the American Atlantic coast. The reaction to the rebellion in the colonies, the 1776 invasion fleet, left America a Uranus-marked land. The threat came from another Uranus marked land–Great Britain– arriving as invasion symbols in the North American Colonies on New York's Long Island.

The actual July 12, 1776, invasion landing sites by British General Howe's fleet occurred under a Uranus line only recently made relevant on the map of the newly established, United States of America, on July 4, 1776. The Declaration of Independence, producing that horoscope-inspired map declared that,

> The history of the present King of Great Britain is a History of repeated Injuries and Usurpations, all having in direct Object the Establishment of an absolute

Tyranny over these States. To prove this, let Facts be submitted to a candid World.

The US founding document continues, listing eighteen specific indictments against King George III concluding with

> In every stage of these Oppressions we have Petitioned for Redress in the most humble Terms: Our repeated Petitions have been answered only by repeated Injury. A Prince, whose Character is thus marked by every act which may define a Tyrant, is unfit to be the Ruler of a free People. (US Declaration of Independence, 1776).

This was a radical denunciation. It was open rebellion, believed in and signed by fifty-six men, presented as representing the People they served. Beyond a doubt, George III triggered the American Revolution with his policies and military actions. The war he triggered synchronized with the discovery of Uranus on March 13, 1781. This Zeitgeist established the idea of open rebellion against inflexible authority as a viable option to astonished onlookers. Freedom movements took root and established themselves in many places in the world and with the British king's defeat and his armies' surrender at Yorktown, Virginia, on October 19, 1781 the option was vindicated.

Another important astrological connection we can make is the fact that another Uranus line, the US Uranus NADIR-angle line, its placement also calculated and set down using the July 4 Declaration of Independence horoscope, sweeps along 3° West 09', 128 miles west of London, embracing the birthplace of King George III.

These 128 miles are considered close for a major US planet line, which has a conservative reach of six degrees or 300 miles east and west of its center. Falling within the range of being born within this zone were many notable players who took sides in the rebellion. Many of the leading colonial and European players of the American Revolution are on a list that includes such chief luminaries as the immigrant firebrands to America, John Paul Jones and Thomas Paine, the British prime minister Lord North, who officiated over the war for Britain, and of course King George III of Britain.

Continuing through France, the Uranus line also cast widely and swept up the birthplaces of French military advisor Marquis de Lafayette, arms dealer Pierre-Augustin Caron de Beaumarchais, French Foreign Minister Comte de Vergennes (responsible for the French Treaty after the American victory at Saratoga), and Louis XVI of France. These astrologically credentialed, major players in the American Revolutionary War were all tied together in the script, "certain things like to happen together," seemingly qualified by the geography of where they were born. We have seen the possibility of deeper not on the map ties in King George III's horoscope. There is no other clear cause-and-effect relationships binding these people together into one script and onto one stage. Further unpacking shows other ties to the US horoscope that are *not on the map*.

A Rodden Rated C horoscope for Lafayette shows his Sun in Virgo, while his Moon (22° Gemini 14') is almost precisely on the US Mars (21° Gemini 22'). Given that this is a C-rated horoscope, this last significant link may not hold. Yet, multiple other ties are clearly there (his Uranus at 21° Pisces 32' retro) even if the time of birth is off. This astrology link to the American cause, to its people, for whom he is a hero may be enough to upgrade his Rodden Rating.

Map 3. Showing the Uranus line relationship between England and its thirteen American colonies.

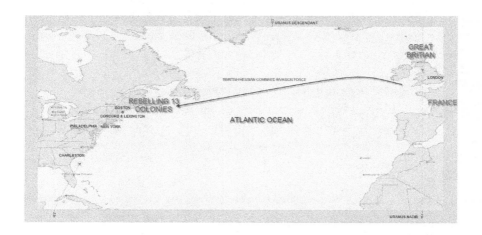

In this map of the east and west sides of the North Atlantic region, two US horoscope Uranus lines are seen marking the British Isles and the thirteen states of the newly declared United States of America. There was a geographic/symbolic relationship *not on the map* of conventional thinking set in place with America's Declaration of Independence.

Not only was Uranus a new planet in 1781, synchronizing with a particular Zeitgeist of new ideals, but it was later found by astronomers to be a planet that broke long-believed astronomical rules of the motion of planets through the solar system, of how planets fit into and perform in that solar system. Uranus orbits on its side, with its pole tilted 98 degrees, pointed at the Solar System's Sun, instead of, like the other planets, orbiting perpendicular to it! Uranus, in short, was in rebellion against the established order in the Solar System, and that rebellion was written largely in the sky!

During the 130 years of the Enlightenment, European thinkers, particularly those born in England and France, imagined and wrote that humanity could be improved through revolution, through breaking with the accustomed, entrenched, *stale* traditions. Thomas Paine, born within the sweep of the Uranus line through Britain on February 9, 1737, was the author of *Common Sense* (anonymously published on January 10, 1776). In addition to this placement marking him Uranian in the 13 Colonies, he was born a Uranus-ruled Sun Aquarian, with his Moon in Gemini, driving the US Mars–Uranus. Lois Rodden gives Thomas Paine a C-Rodden Rated horoscope set on January 29, 1737, for the Julian calendar and February 9, 1737, via the Gregorian calendar. Words from Paine's *The Crisis* comes through time to today, still ringing fresh rebellion in the ears of those who rebel for just change.

> These are the times that try men's souls: The summer soldier and the sunshine patriot will, in this crisis, shrink from the service of his country; but he that stands it now, deserves the love and thanks of man and woman. (Shapiro, 2006)

Paine's words were read to the troops of George Washington's hard-pressed army, at Valley Forge, days before the epic morale-raising American victory at the Battle of Trenton on December 26, 1776. It joined as script to the remarkable story unfolding, establishing the iconic image of Washington's famous crossing of the Delaware.

Brown University's Pulitzer-winning (1993) historian Gordon S. Wood, born in Concord, Massachusetts, under the Atlantic coast running US Uranus line in 1933) called *Common Sense*, "The most incendiary and popular pamphlet of the entire revolutionary era." This spirit of rebellion, describing the times, inserted itself into how one lived life *free* day-to-day; it motivated the people politically, while also synchronizing new discoveries, habits, and spawned innovations and pressured for balanced, just laws. People like Thomas Paine, Uranus marked, embodied armed rebellion.

Looking back at the record, modern astrologers would easily associate Uranus as the symbol of the US colonial rebellion against English laws. Think of the play Hamiliton. The American Revolution came at great risk to the colonials. England was one of the greatest military powers on Earth—a superpower!

The American and French Revolutions synchronized with a great turning of the world upside down. France, England's nemesis and another superpower, faced its own overturn on the heels of the Americans winning their cause, with French help. It was as if collectively the French people caught a contagion that had spread from the US shores, with their returning navy, to French shores. The winds driving events in both revolutions were ideals, the heady concepts of equality, freedom, and liberty. These words fanned and spread the flames—the spirit of the times—the Zeitgeist.

It remains for astrologers to master the lessons of history, read the signs, and connect Uranus with these powerful words—equality, freedom, and liberty and apply them to the present and future. The popularization of these ideals, synchronizing with the emergence of Uranus into reality, was passionately debated, desperately embraced, and explosively acted out during the Age of Enlightenment. This period centered around the planet's discovery on March 13, 1781.

Remember your history. Patrick Henry's choice of words, arguing for Virginia to commit soldiers to the cause of revolution, were a bellwether in 1775 when he said, "Give me liberty, or give me death!" That liberty was secured from Britain on the Yorktown, Virginia, battlefield on October 19, 1781. There is that word *liberty* used like a match to ignite events.

KEY WIP BRANCHES: 35° NORTH & SOUTH ~ 6° NORTH & SOUTH
10° EAST ~ 103° EAST ~ 77° WEST ~ 169° WEST ~ 3° WEST

The word liberty is one of those things that like to happen together when there is rebellion. Then again, there is the word idealized in the Declaration of Independence, "Endowed by their Creator with certain unalienable Rights, that among these are Life, Liberty, and the Pursuit of Happiness." And for the French, a decade and a half later on December 5, 1790, the Uranian zeitgeist reality crystallized in Robespierre's catchy motto, "Liberté, Egalité, Fraternité!" Think Ho Chi Minh's declaration of Vietnamese Independence in 1945.

Inspired by events in France, embracing the French Revolution's triad of Uranian words, Haitians embraced the same Uranus ideals as their American and French brethren for their own revolutionary cause, under the leadership of Toussaint L'Ouverture in 1791. And if you consulted a map of the period, would there have been any astrological mark of distinction, any US *WIP* qualities, running through Haiti's geography? Astrology maps reveal that answer to be yes.

For example, an astrologer can read Uranus in a nation's horoscope and see its seasons of rebellion, the when and where of them. Sooner or later, as a part of maturing, a violent revolution or some corresponding Uranian event (discovery, innovation, or breakthrough to a solution), breaks out in every country. Recently, a dramatic demonstration of this played out in Turkey during 2016–2017, when the epic transit of slow-moving Neptune moved to cross Turkey's Uranus position, placed in horoscope at 13° Pisces 54' retrograde, at the zenith of the chart.

This very public, attempted coup synchronized around Friday, July 15, 2016. In the US, the coup events were of major concern in Washington, DC, because they happened to a major strategic partner. Fethullah Gulen, a Turkish cleric, one of the world's most important Muslim figures, was accused by Turkey of being the leader of the coup attempt. He is living in the US, in the heart of the *WIP* running through Pennsylvania.

This coup event was forecastable as far back as the Arab Spring (2010–2011). Its reading would have been accomplished by monitoring the transits of those planets that were capable of timing meaningful synchronizations to the Turkish horoscope. We learn a great deal when we take a backward look on the time cycles of the *'outer planets'*, using astrological tools capable of revealing what is *not on the map* of contemporary reality.

KEY WIP BRANCHES: 35° NORTH & SOUTH ~ 6° NORTH & SOUTH
10° EAST ~ 103° EAST ~ 77° WEST ~ 169° WEST ~ 3° WEST

The completion of the great stimulating cycles of the US Uranus express with force, as dramatic as any of Earth's four seasons can. For the US Uranus cycles have in my research results usually accompanied war for the US. The most spectacular example of this is what synchronized under the first Return of Uranus to its original place.

A Return means that Uranus's eighty-four-year circuit around the sun cycle resets to its original position at 8° Gemini 55' or to a 0-aspect and starts over again. In astrological parlance, you now recognize this as a *conjunction* or a 0-degree aspect relationship, a refocusing in any horoscope. America's horoscope experienced the first-ever Uranus return to 8° Gemini 55' in June 1860, and in its retrograde period, synchronized the union falling apart. The back-and-forth movement over the sensitive Uranus point over the next ten months through April 1861, synchronized the firing on Fort Sumter in Charleston Harbor just west of the US descendant Uranus line. Just as profound was this synchronization.

> *Four score and seven years ago our fathers brought forth on this continent, a new nation, conceived in Liberty, and dedicated to the proposition that all men are created equal.*
> (President Abraham Lincoln, "Gettysburg Address," November 19, 1863)

American Civil War—April 1861 to April 1865

A score is equal to twenty years. Four score equals eighty years. Add to that sum the seven years and you get eighty-seven years from the time of Lincoln's speech to the day of the Declaration of Independence. The year 1776 + 87 years gives 1863. That year timed one of the greatest battles in US history.

Uranus had moved, in its peculiar orbit, around the sun and returned to where it was at 8° Gemini 55' on July 4, 1776. *Remember, converting this establishment moment into a map, an Astro*Carto*Graphy® map, the skilled astrologer can also narrow down the where of any past or future Uranus event for the US. This geographic narrowing can be very precise, within tens of miles, or closer, revealing awesome intelligence!*

KEY WIP BRANCHES: 35° NORTH & SOUTH ~ 6° NORTH & SOUTH
10° EAST ~ 103° EAST ~ 77° WEST ~ 169° WEST ~ 3° WEST

Earlier, I pointed out that during the Persian Gulf War, Operation Desert (1991), part of the US command structure operated out of a US base in Bahrain at 50° East 35', 41 miles east of the Partial Solar Eclipse-activated US Pluto line. The ComUSNAVCENT, for the Iraq War, operated from onboard ship. The land-based command was in Riyadh (NAVCENT-Riyadh) at 46° E 43', some 200 miles west of the line. During WWII, General Eisenhower commanded the Normandy Invasion of Europe from Portsmouth, UK, in the teeth of the US Uranus Ic zone.

The point here is that America's astrological baseline set down in 1776, almost 175 years old in 1944, could have contributed valuable intelligence to Eisenhower's planning. It could have been deployed as a tool, measuring where and when the geographic parameters of the battlefield would have been optimal. And that this could have been accomplished with a great deal of accuracy! To read things *not on the map* before events required an astrological mind-set recognizing what a solar eclipse to the US Pluto might mean in 1991. *I should point out that Pluto was* not on the map *of astrologers until after 1930, when its reality was discovered, it closely synchronized with the US Standard Oil Company of California (Socal) 1932 discovery of oil in Bahrain, at 50° East 32'3" in the Persian Gulf.*

I digress! Let's go back to Uranus in Civil War times. Those certain Uranian things, that liked to happen together, gathered for the US under its Uranus lines during the historically important Civil War trauma for the US people. Consider the following astrological facts about place for the US.

President Abraham Lincoln, born (a B-Rodden Rating on February 12, 1809) with an Aquarian Sun, thus Uranus-ruled, was newly sworn in as president on March 4, 1861. Lincoln's predecessor, President James Buchanan had previously ordered an attempt to reinforce and supply the Fort Sumter, which failed. So when Lincoln came into office, March 4, 1861, that urgent problem was waiting as one of his first executive actions, waiting for his immediate attention as commander-in-chief.

He, his advisors, and the confederates were aware that reinforcement and resupply of Fort Sumter was the spark that would ignite armed conflict. A Commander-in-Chief, Lincoln had to address the unresolved, vital military question of whether to reinforce or resupply the fort. He did so on March 9, in a letter to Commanding General of the US Army Winfield Scott. Think Mexican-American War.

In the first month of his administration (March 4 to April 9), Lincoln argued back and forth with his secretary of state William H. Steward over the wisdom of resupplying Fort Sumter. The secretary argued that it would be seen as a provocation and start a civil war, which, as it turned out, was an existential challenge to the existence of the US.

Secretary Seward stated, in writing, that control of Fort Sumter should be transferred to the South Carolinians. But in early 1861, few places made as much strategic sense, for controlling at the start of war, as did the Charleston, South Carolina, fort. Aware today, that foreknowledge of where and when a war would breakout, to within ninety miles, is possible, it seems certain such uncanny, strategic astrological intelligence would have been highly prized by President Lincoln at that time. After all, it is alleged that the First Lady conducted seances in the White House, during the Civil War. Think Willie Lincoln's death.

All the astrological planet components were discovered (Uranus and Neptune) and in place for the astrologers of that era to have teased out the pattern constituting the WIP. But it would have been forward thinking, even revolutionary, to conceive of and then embrace such a tool. An army of mathematicians would have had to have been deployed in 1861 to calculate all the relocations to reveal the A*C*G gestalt. Today it's simply a push of send on a computer keyboard. The first shot of the US Civil War came from a mortar fired from Fort Johnson, at Windmill Point, on James Island, South Carolina.

Fort Johnson was in the harbor of Charleston, within range and sight of Fort Sumter. In the broader view of the US Astro*Carto*Graphy® (A*C*G) map, the city of Charleston and the fort are less than ninety miles northwest of the US Uranus DESCENDANT line. This is considered close for a major planet line in the A*C*G scheme. This astrologically measured line remains permanently, for the life of the nation, off the coast of the Carolinas in the open waters of the Atlantic.

Lincoln was not the first and won't be the last president to take office and find an existential crisis waiting. I can't help but think that Lincoln would have made different decisions, with a different feeling of sensitivity and urgency, had he known what Fort Sumter represented astrologically and geographically. If he knew the meaning of the Uranus symbol in the nation's horoscope and its map pattern, as well as his own connection to Uranus, what then? If he were aware of a *WIP* reality, would he have acted differently?

Map 4. Uranus line along South Carolina coast and Charleston.

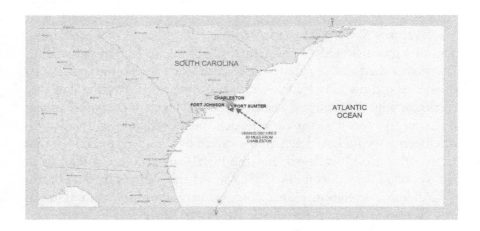

Under that Uranus line, running the US eastern coast, there were other flashpoints. But the Carolinas are also marked with emphasis by other horoscope-derived lines that made a strong case, particularly in places (forts) north along the coast of Charleston along 35° North latitude. Specifically, upon close inspection, the yet-undeveloped Fort Fisher at 33° North 58', 62 miles south of the 35th latitude, was a strong candidate. In its favor Fort Fisher was closer to the active Uranus line, 17 miles as opposed to 90 miles away; the politics in North Carolina were not as supercharged as they were in Charleston, with its long history of being in the thick of conflict from revolutionary times. But Fort Fisher would become the lynchpin for Confederate General Lees' army resupply. Pulling in in 1865 forced Lee's surrender. Think Appomattox Surrender.

Fort Fisher was the protection for the waterways leading up to the docks of Wilmington, North Carolina, a place of major strategic importance, especially as the Union blockades took hold. Fort Fisher was not completed in April 1861, as Lincoln struggled with his advisors over the problem of Fort Sumter. During the four years of the Civil War, civilian and military leaders in Washington, DC, would rapidly come to recognize the strategic military importance of the geographic North Carolina-Virginia coastline for America.

Once realized, that insight did not lose its power, to this day, in the minds of US military planners in places like Camp Lejeune, Fort Bragg, Langley Air Force Base, and Norfolk Naval Base Complex. *When you think of North Carolina, think Fort Bragg, that's the biggest American fort and home of the special forces.*

Just speculating, but suppose new Commander-in-Chief Lincoln's foreknowledge of the Uranus Return cycle had him time an occupation of that unfinished Fort Fisher, with his Union forces. Imagine No siege of Petersburg, Battle of the Crater, or Battle of the Wilderness casualties. Think of the movie *Cold Mountain*. Eventually Fort Fisher did develop into the Confederate Gibraltar- the largest earthen fort on Earth, guarding Wilmington, North Carolina, and the main resupply route for Confederate General Lee's army, during much of the Civil War. When Fisher eventually fell, after several attempts by Union forces, Wilmington fell, and with it the South fell.

The specificity of measuring such things *not on any map*, that astrology reveals, is astonishing! It is especially so given the huge numbers, the scale of the Earth, that we must deal with across the US, indeed the entire globe. Consider that the near 25,000-mile circumference size of the Earth, along the equator, is 71 percent water!

When? Where? In a straight line, it is a morass of pinpoints without the astrology map to order it. The US Atlantic coastline is over 2,000 miles long with an astrological Uranus line tracing much of that distance from Maine to the Florida Keys.

These miles can be winnowed down to an even smaller, extremely manageable number, with which to work. In the Age of Computers, the work of astrology becomes exponentially easier. Still, the range of choices is daunting, especially if it remains locked to conventional theories, ways of reasoning reality.

Astrology affirms this and moves the mind further to reveal something extraordinarily different. It reveals that breakthrough in thinking that permits earth-shaking ideas that are *not on the map*. It shows what was previously unknown, considered unknowable, things like *where* the man who would light the fuse launching that first bomb in a war might originate from, perhaps even *when* he was likely born, or *who* might die.

Conventional wisdom argues, how is this sort of knowledge possible? Think Fraud Statute in most city police codes in America. Most importantly, how is it actionable? The importance of July 4, 1776, in terms of astrological philosophy, with the necessary planets in place, was well-known and long celebrated, and available to those who could use it during the Civil War. Freemasons, who understood astrology, operated at the highest levels from the time of the American Revolution. George Washington, James Monroe, Andrew Jackson, and James Polk were all Freemasons leading up to Abraham Lincoln's presidency.

Consider that astrology can narrow numbers and symbols down to represent measurable realities, accurate to within tens of miles. A narrowing to tens of miles around one planet line all around the Earth marks a handful of congenitally marked geographic places along an east-west line. Some of them are remote specks of land amid gargantuan oceans. The American Civil War was fought overseas.

Far from American shores, 3,850 miles away to the east, on June 19, 1864, under another Uranus line, American technologically advanced Union and Confederate warships engaged in a desperate battle in waters off foreign shores. The lightly armored USS *Kearsarge* first blockaded and then battled the CSS *Alabama* off Cherbourg, France, along 1° West 42' longitude and sank the Confederate ship. An angular US Uranus line runs along the 3° West 09' longitude, 87 miles west of the scene of the naval battle.

Within 24 hours of that sea battle, there was a Full Moon at 28° Sagittarius +. As the sea battle took place, the Sun was in late Gemini, timing the annual awakening of the Mars and Uranus expressions of the *WIP* by the Sun's passage. Simultaneously, Uranus was transiting at 25° Gemini 23', still aspecting the two *WIP* Gemini planets. Venus and Mercury were transiting in Gemini as well. Point! The battle was astrologically synchronized in time (Gemini planets) and in place (Uranus line). What other way of seeing could have seen meaning in that battle far in advance of time?

This irony speaks volumes. Almost exactly another four score and seven years later (1860 + 87 = 1947), in the season of the second Uranus

Return in US history, another epic war, another epic battle staged under a Uranus line involving the US took place. *Remember that the start of the Civil War was synchronized, under a US Uranus line, by the first US Uranus Return, coupled with a Mars Return on April 12, 1861.*

As transiting Mars approached its seventy-fifth Return in the US horoscope, crossing the Uranus position, America entered WWI, landing its Doughboys on the coast of France at St. Nazaire on June 26, 1917. St. Nazaire is located at 2° West 12'31"! On June 6, 1944, also under the same Uranus line, Americans fought and died in the waters off Cherbourg, France. Remember how Uranus synchronized the epic Civil War battle between the USS *Kearsarge* and the CSS *Alabama*.

The June 6, 1944 event was the Normandy Invasion of Europe (D-Day). *Let me remind you here that the US Uranus at 8° Gemini 55' in the horoscope converts to an Astro*Carto*Graphy (A*C*G) line along 3° West 09' longitude.* General Eisenhower, commanding general of the invasion, was headquartered in Portsmouth, UK, at 1° West 05', well within the Uranus zone.

On June 6, 1944, with the Sun in Gemini, transiting Uranus was at 9° Gemini 18'. History records that the port of Cherbourg, France, the object of Operation Overlord's Normandy Invasion was finally captured by the US and Allied Forces on June 26, 1944.

As I have said, for the US, certain geography across the Earth is permanently marked by three planets, each with four different major geographic zones of focus around the, where their different qualities synergistically have a pronounced angular emphasis as the WIP. It should be noted here that there are also east-west *WIP* effects along certain latitude lines, such as 6° North and South and 35° North and South latitudes, which time and again, prove critically important for the US geopolitically and militarily. The existence of these congenital *WIP* planet lines, Mars, Uranus and Neptune, shaping the US experience in geographically identified places, can be demonstrated as fact, and these facts can be made *actionable*!

This astrological reality doesn't need to work perfectly, just work better than what has been on offer for centuries. It must be evolved and made current with the other great changes happening in the world of today. Through mathematical manipulation, these astrological facts can be managed in a way to show relationships, which are not found on any other map of reality.

KEY WIP BRANCHES: 35° NORTH & SOUTH ~ 6° NORTH & SOUTH
10° EAST ~ 103° EAST ~ 77° WEST ~ 169° WEST ~ 3° WEST

That mathematical ability to articulate these facts *can* be deployed to research past relevance and anticipate or determine future places of military experience for the nation. *I am not overstating my point. All relations such as these were laid down, like a ship's keel, on July 4, 1776, 4:47 p.m. in Philadelphia, Pennsylvania.*

This deserves repeating. It remains for each generation of astrologers to connect and repurpose Uranus and the other *WIP* planets with fitting language, the words of the day conveying the newly evolved consciousness captured in the stories describing events and experiences. Like the words that connect to the ideals set down in 1776 and 1787— equality, freedom, and liberty. The popularization of these ideals, synchronizing with Uranus's emergence into reality, were passionately debated, desperately embraced, and explosively acted out, during the Enlightenment and Revolutionary years. This nature, frozen in the US character, returns cyclically, in new garb.

It needs repeating that there was a period of years that centered around the planet's discovery on March 13, 1781. Inspired by events in France and embracing the French Revolution's triad of Uranian words, Haitians too embraced the Uranus ideal of liberty for their own revolutionary cause under the leadership of Toussaint L'Ouverture in 1791. Imagine?

What if a reader of those times had consulted the newly formed US astrology horoscope and its derivative Astro*Carto*Graphy® map in real time. During the period, would they have been struck by any astrological mark of distinction, any US *WIP* qualities, running through Haiti's geography? It would have been clear as a bell that a Mars line ran diagonally, through the island of Haiti—San Domingo, passing just fifty-three miles southeast of Port-au-Prince.

The fact of the matter was this that even then, the US was connected, or wired as is said today, to events in Haiti, to the whole of the Earth, to every place, every event, and even every person. *This is the truest meaning of the astrological understanding of Neptune!*

Neptune—An Outer Planet

—the Immense, Compelling Mass Collective Pressure to Flow with and Go Along with Collective and Cultural Trends

KEY WIP BRANCHES: 35° NORTH & SOUTH ~ 6° NORTH & SOUTH
10° EAST ~ 103° EAST ~ 77° WEST ~ 169° WEST ~ 3° WEST

Neptune's discovery on September 24, 1846, ushered in a different zeitgeist from that of the Uranian pantheon of ideas, ideas which we can see, in hindsight, ignited an enlightenment and an industrial age. Neptune synchronized with the sense of a greatly expanded universe of interconnectedness on a whole new order. The 1781 Uranian age of electric shocks was quickly adjusted to by collectives globally, whose inspired members actually harnessed and molded electricity into the inventions of an Electromechanical (mass production) Age (1840–1940).

It was an age meant to serve the masses. In the US, a myriad of things electromechanical evolved molding the culture, synchronizing with Neptune's addition to the map of a flood of things in existence in the universe. Neptune's feeling of intoxication joined with new worldly faddish things like the telegraph, which was a Uranian invention but with Neptune's predisposal to make ties to the universal. As if in a dream, now communication with distant places could be tied together, shortening the time necessary to share important and even strategic information. Presidents could speak to their generals on distant battlefields almost instantaneously.

Electricity (Uranus) was made into glamorous (Neptune) tools. People sensed their lives moved faster in this world. It was a world that ushered in a miraculous age of telecommunications, innovation connecting *everything* together into a vast *unified field* at speeds and by means, hard to believe.

Technology was harnessed to serve the needs of America's growing collective. Promethean/Uranian/Neptunian inventions improved human life, but some of the improvements seemed pure glamor. For instance, like the daguerreotype (photograph) was when it was first introduced into the US after 1840. Photography gradually grew in popularity in the US through the 1850s and exploded during the Civil War years.

In today's world where nearly everyone has some form of ID card and can visually shop *online* for purchases, it is hard to imagine what a world without the photographic process would be like. Compared to today's world, before the invention of the photographic process, humanity was blind. Neptune is at once a delusion and an enlightenment.

Using a daguerreotype camera, the people of the post-1840 age were, in the US, for the first time able to create unimpeachable witnesses to their existence, to their individualism and to their life experiences.

There was now an unimpeachable witness to historical events. The camera offered a new standard of fact to the world—photographic proof!

The invention sharpened the eyes to the folly of glamorizing warfare. The camera offered the average citizen access to the graphic images of death and destruction, captured on the battlefields of the US Civil War. These images reached a stunned public through the journals and newspapers of the day.

Armed with such wizard-like power in the run-up to the Civil War, there was an increasing sense of superiority developing in the hearts of Americans. Americans were already exterminating native people and held slaves. They built upon their myth of the innovator culture acting negatively toward nonwhite people of other, less-respected traditions.

US government practices fostered this belief by promoting land rushes by European immigrants and through propagandizing utopian (Neptune) ideas (Uranus) like Manifest Destiny. Such attitudes drove the land grabs of Indian Treaty lands during the late 1800s. This spurred racism against indigenous North American tribal cultures and spurred their subsequent rebellions, throughout the US heartland and beyond.

Neptune's discovery synchronized with the hot debates in the US on human compassion vs. victimization. Neptune, the key planet of the *WIP*, found its issues played out in the public arena. The world saw the birth of communism, Marx and Engels *The Communist Manifesto* in 1848, it synchronized with this *not-on-the-map* planet's discovery.

The US mainland experienced massive expansion during the Neptune discovery. The Mexican-American War's beginning synchronized with the zeitgeist of Neptune's discovery date on September 24, 1846. The US Congress declared war with Mexico on May 13, 1846. Geography gained through the Mexican War brought massive spoils—the annexation of California, Arizona, New Mexico, and Texas—from Mexico and legitimized with the war—ending Treaty of Guadalupe-Hidalgo (1848).

Such stories from those times go to the heart of things Neptunian, Koestler's "certain things that like to happen together." US government pamphleteering campaigns encouraged the epic migrations across the Great Plains. There was a great rush for gold in 1849, then another for silver in 1858.

KEY WIP BRANCHES: 35° NORTH & SOUTH ~ 6° NORTH & SOUTH
10° EAST ~ 103° EAST ~ 77° WEST ~ 169° WEST ~ 3° WEST

Lastly, there was a rush for living space and opportunity, with the westward expansion. These events occurred in the decades after the Mexican-American War. Land grabs substantially increased the population and exponentially increased the size of the US.

Great dreams were being pursued en masse. Neptune is quintessentially about dreaming and utopias. There was glamor in these adventures. The US government actively encouraged this glamorizing.

Synchronized with the Neptune discovery, there was a widespread sense, in America, that people of an advanced culture should rule all. It crystallized in the zeitgeist as *manifest destiny* and continued as chattel slavery. The US has never fully recovered from the consequences of that delusionary contagion of beliefs.

Neptune is very prominent in the US horoscope and like Uranus's geographic A*C*G emphasis to the US Atlantic coastline, Neptune geographically has one of its four angular lines, running north/south through much of the eastern part of the US mainland, along 76° West 50'; in this case, where Neptune is said to be on the MIDHEAVEN Angle.

The next chapters introduce astrology horoscopes and maps that will visually illuminate all these insights on a grand, unified international field.

Chapter 4

Alignment of American Ideals with the WIP

So far, we know that three planets make up the *WIP*. They are Mars, Uranus, and Neptune. We have seen the US horoscope distilled down to these three planet symbols and we've seen some geographic Astro*Carto*Graphy (A*C*G)® maps that result from the distilled horoscope baseline. Each planet making up the *WIP* has a number degree and zodiac sign assigned to it. These are the planets' addresses in the zodiac wheel.

Every horoscope has a complete zodiac of twelve signs. All zodiacs are a perfect circle of 360-degrees. It is a neat system. For the US:

- Uranus is at 8° Gemini 55', or 68, nearly 69 degrees through a 360-degree cycle.
- the address of Mars is at 21° Gemini 22' or 81, nearly 82 degrees into that circle.
- the final planet Neptune has its address at 22° Virgo 25' or 172, nearly 173 degrees through the zodiac.

Each of these three planets has a relationship to one another. These relationships are called *aspects*, measured in specific degree units. In terms of the *WIP*, we are only concerned with units of 0°, 90°, 180°, and 270° aspects, which denote angularity. These addresses and their aspects allow every horoscope ever made to be compared with the US *WIP*.

Every horoscope ever calculated in this unified system is relevant. Each horoscope connects to events and is part of the whole.

Using basic astrological facts, all manner of reports, important documents, history-making events, the horoscopes of other countries, every American citizen, and the remaining people of the world (all eight billion on the planet) can all be compared and related through their horoscopes and juxtaposed with the US horoscope and its *WIP*. *You just have to keep track of the significant moments, beyond birth, as they come into existence.* My intention here is to discuss how things like the ideals set down in the US Declaration of Independence and Constitution plug into and drive the *WIP*. The Constitution *is* the US.

It is the second most important document after the Declaration of Independence. Anything else that shapes the American identity is dictated and *subsumed* by these two great overarching structures. The *WIP* serves the US Constitution as a part of the nation's chief executive and congressional military expression. The Congress is given the power to wage war abroad, in areas ironically marked by the *WIP*. The president, as commander-in-chief has the power to wage war in domestic situations and command American armies, in areas marked by the *WIP*. This requires an understanding of the WIP tool.

So far, I have given a wide ranging narrative of the expression and a core understanding of the *WIP's* strategic importance throughout this primer. I will continue to do so in the subsequent series of related books. I will go to great lengths to connect the *WIP* dots tracing across international stages.

Imagine demonstrating a method that connects people and events to specific places, for example, a soldier born in Oklahoma, trains at Fort Bragg, North Carolina, fights and dies on a battlefield in Iraq or Afghanistan, all places along the same latitude, places thousands of miles apart, east-west with little deviation. How does such a situation occur time and time again? How does conventional wisdom explain the facts of that reality? Coincidence? It is more than coincidence - astrologically specific people are connected to specific geographic places in straight lines across the Earth!

KEY WIP BRANCHES: 35° NORTH & SOUTH ~ 6° NORTH & SOUTH
10° EAST ~ 103° EAST ~ 77° WEST ~ 169° WEST ~ 3° WEST

Let's not forget about the strategic power of astrological timing, specific people can be synchronized using their birth horoscope to connect with events of interest to the US on specific stages. Think military personnel! Think ambassadors! The WIP universally measures the relationship between people, events, and places. Moving forward, this process of connecting to and consciously choosing what and who to set on conflict stages, represented as dots across the Earth will remain my key methodology for making demonstrations.

As I said, after the Declaration of Independence, the most important US document, representing the ideals of the people and intentions of the founders, was the Constitution. It was the Constitution which empowered the high ideals set out by the Declaration of Independence. Because of this fact, the horoscope of the Constitution becomes of paramount importance on this journey to understand the *WIP,* that signature to the US military and its *civilian* control. A comprehensive unpacking of the Constitution's ties to the *WIP* needs to be made.

September 17, 1787, at 11:29 a.m., in Philadelphia, Pennsylvania, is the date used (and celebrated) for the historic signing of the US Constitution. The Rodden Rating system gives the data a dirty data (DD) status, because of discrepancies surrounding the timing. The date (day) itself, however, is not in dispute, neither is the place (Philadelphia). *I remind you here that I use and have unwavering confidence in the 4:47 p.m. timed horoscope (Rodden Rated-C) for the national horoscope because I have followed the domestic astrological debate in the US, made my selection and faithfully tested it for thirty-five years. Faithfully following consensus history, I have produced prediction results which support my position. I stake my ground in facts-common and not on the map. The WIP is the product of those three and a half decades of inquiry.*

Back to the Constitution's relationship to the Declaration of Independence (DOI) horoscope. Once calculated, the first thing that should catch the eye is the placement of the Sun symbol in the Constitution's horoscope at 24° Virgo 39'. *Observe,* in the next horoscope illustration, that the Constitution's Sun placement is quite near the US Neptune placement at 22° Virgo 25', in the Declaration horoscope.

Data 7. Here is the 10th house placement of the Virgo Sun in the Constitution horoscope.

☉ | Sun | Virgo | 10th | 24°♍39'

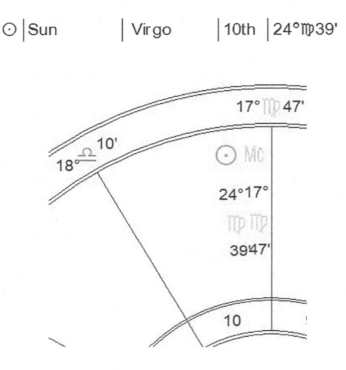

This shows that the Constitution's Sun placement, at 24° Virgo 39', its power, must always be considered through the lens of the DOI Neptunian idealism. That Sun precisely aligns to the MIDHEAVEN MH/MC of the US horoscope, which is at 24° Virgo 46'. The MH of any Mundane horoscope symbolizes those achievements, fame, goals, powers, and responsibilities of a country, and the sign of the MH in Virgo emphasizes the *what*; in this instance Virgo ♍ astrologically corresponds with the military prowess of US armies.

The Sun symbol in astrology corresponds to the animating spirit, the life-force of the entity. It is also the authority, the heart center, commanding blood, brain, and the circulation of power throughout the entity. *Keep in mind* that the WIP Neptune placement is quite close to the Constitution-Sun placement. Understood astrologically, the Neptune of the DOI horoscope subsumes the Sun of the Constitution horoscope. The Constitution is bound to the ideals of the DOI; it animates those ideals.

The US Constitution represents the authority, blood, brain, and circulation of the power of the American citizenry! The Sun in a Mundane (national, political) horoscope is also the leadership; in the US system that is the chief executive, president, also known as the commander-in-chief. With the constitution in place, and powers shared out, the country acquired an operating creed based upon its founding ideals.

The Constitution says so, in words, right from the beginning. "WE THE PEOPLE OF THE UNITED STATES, IN ORDER TO form a more perfect Union, establish Justice, insure domestic Tranquility, provide for the common defense, promote the general Welfare, and secure the Blessings of Liberty to ourselves and our Posterity, do ordain and establish this Constitution for the United States of America."

Horoscope 6. Of the US Constitution.

The freedom won by the Revolutionary War now had its blueprint.

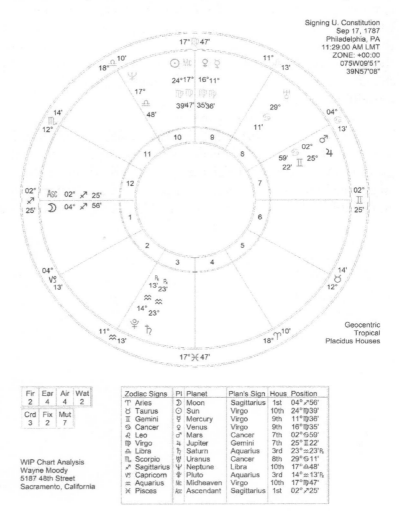

Signing U. Constitution
Sep 17, 1787
Philadelphia, PA
11:29:00 AM LMT
ZONE: +00:00
075W09'51"
39N57'08"

Geocentric
Tropical
Placidus Houses

Fir	Ear	Air	Wat
2	4	4	2

Crd	Fix	Mut
3	2	7

WIP Chart Analysis
Wayne Moody
5187 48th Street
Sacramento, California

Zodiac Signs		Pl	Planet	Plan's Sign	Hous	Position
♈	Aries	☽	Moon	Sagittarius	1st	04° ♐ 56'
♉	Taurus	☉	Sun	Virgo	10th	24° ♍ 39'
♊	Gemini	☿	Mercury	Virgo	9th	11° ♍ 36'
♋	Cancer	♀	Venus	Virgo	9th	16° ♍ 35'
♌	Leo	♂	Mars	Cancer	7th	02° ♋ 59'
♍	Virgo	♃	Jupiter	Gemini	7th	25° ♊ 22'
♎	Libra	♄	Saturn	Aquarius	3rd	23° ♒ 23' ℞
♏	Scorpio	♅	Uranus	Cancer	8th	29° ♋ 11'
♐	Sagittarius	♆	Neptune	Libra	10th	17° ♎ 48'
♑	Capricorn	♇	Pluto	Aquarius	3rd	14° ♒ 13' ℞
♒	Aquarius	Mc	Midheaven	Virgo	10th	17° ♍ 47'
♓	Pisces	Asc	Ascendant	Sagittarius	1st	02° ♐ 25'

Novice 2 Wheel

KEY WIP BRANCHES: 35° NORTH & SOUTH ~ 6° NORTH & SOUTH
10° EAST ~ 103° EAST ~ 77° WEST ~ 169° WEST ~ 3° WEST

Horoscope 7. Once again, the WIP pattern in the US horoscope.

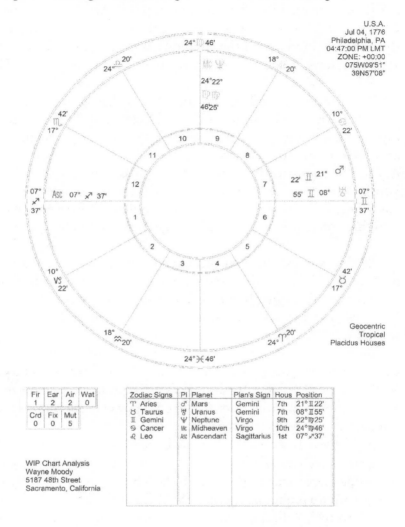

U.S.A.
Jul 04, 1776
Philadelphia, PA
04:47:00 PM LMT
ZONE: +00:00
075W09'51"
39N57'08"

Geocentric
Tropical
Placidus Houses

Fir	Ear	Air	Wat
1	2	2	0

Crd	Fix	Mut
0	0	5

Zodiac Signs		Pl	Planet	Plan's Sign	Hous	Position
♈	Aries	♂	Mars	Gemini	7th	21° ♊ 22'
♉	Taurus	♅	Uranus	Gemini	7th	08° ♊ 55'
♊	Gemini	♆	Neptune	Virgo	9th	22° ♍ 25'
♋	Cancer	Mc	Midheaven	Virgo	10th	24° ♍ 46'
♌	Leo	Asc	Ascendant	Sagittarius	1st	07° ♐ 37'

WIP Chart Analysis
Wayne Moody
5187 48th Street
Sacramento, California

Novice 2 Wheel

KEY WIP BRANCHES: 35° NORTH & SOUTH ~ 6° NORTH & SOUTH
10° EAST ~ 103° EAST ~ 77° WEST ~ 169° WEST ~ 3° WEST

The president, empowered as the Sun symbol in this horoscope, swears an oath established by the Constitution, Article II, Section One, Clause 8, to "solemnly swear (or affirm) that I will faithfully execute the Office of President of the United States, and will to the best of my ability preserve, protect, and defend the Constitution of the United States."

The relevance of all this to the *WIP* is that an interpretation of the beliefs and ideals set down in the Declaration are supposed to be executed (preserved, protected, and defended) by the president through assigned executive powers given that elected person in the Constitution. Again, the Constitution's horoscope Sun on the DOI 10th house MIDHEAVEN angle, 24° Virgo 46', empowers the president and other government leaders. The Constitution stipulates a separation of powers into three branches: The executive, legislative, and judiciary branches.

Within a week, the Constitutional Convention reached a quorum on May 25, 1787, selecting George Washington as the president of the Convention. Transiting Jupiter was precisely aligned with the transiting Sun that day at 3°–4° Gemini. Take a moment with the astrology reasoning.

Jupiter signifies growth, and the Sun is authority and power. Put the two together you get a growth in authority and power. Who grows? Well, certainly President Washington's social position, his renown grew. Washington is famous for not abusing the power given him. He set the standard for presidential decorum.

Reader, you have enough astrological information here to see symbolically what was at the core of events. The symbolism provides the insight that the people, represented by Jupiter in the horoscope are the body public of the nation (Jupiter being the US ASC ruler). These people sought growth in their collective identity and rebelled against the limitations of the governing system then in place, the shopworn Articles of Confederation (the first US Constitution). The Articles were the power sharing arrangements that united theThirteen British Colonies through the Revolutionary War. This is seen in Jupiter crossing through Gemini toward the Uranus and Mars positions of the US horoscope *WIP*, during the Constitutional Convention. Jupiter corresponds with this attempt at fairness, an expansion of the American franchise. However, it fell short, again, when it came to indigious Americans and slaves, mostly from African origins. Moving forward, this would prove an Achilles heel for the US.

Horoscope 8. In this distilled horoscope for the Constitution you see the placement of the Sun near the MIDHEAVEN angle in square (90 degrees) to Jupiter in the 7th House.

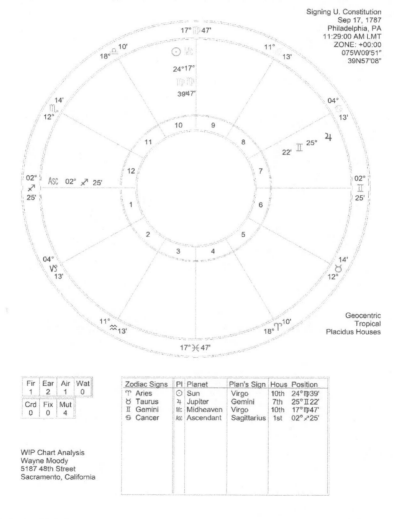

Signing U. Constitution
Sep 17, 1787
Philadelphia, PA
11:29:00 AM LMT
ZONE: +00:00
075W09'51"
39N57'08"

Geocentric
Tropical
Placidus Houses

Fir	Ear	Air	Wat
1	2	1	0

Crd	Fix	Mut
0	0	4

Zodiac Signs		Pl	Planet	Plan's Sign	Hous	Position
♈	Aries	☉	Sun	Virgo	10th	24°♍39'
♉	Taurus	♃	Jupiter	Gemini	7th	25°♊22'
♊	Gemini	Mc	Midheaven	Virgo	10th	17°♍47'
♋	Cancer	Asc	Ascendant	Sagittarius	1st	02°♐25'

WIP Chart Analysis
Wayne Moody
5187 48th Street
Sacramento, California

Novice 2 Wheel

KEY WIP BRANCHES: 35° NORTH & SOUTH ~ 6° NORTH & SOUTH
10° EAST ~ 103° EAST ~ 77° WEST ~ 169° WEST ~ 3° WEST

That Bill of Rights, the first ten Amendments to the Constitution were ratified on December 15, 1791, when transiting Mars was precisely on the US Neptune, synchronized with the will of the people. On Revolutionary War veteran Daniel Shays tombstone it reads, *"Leader of the 1786–1787 Shays' Rebellion that influenced the creation of the US Constitution."* It is one of the nation's and the people's' founding principles that *"whenever any form of Government becomes destructive of these Ends, it is the Right of the People to alter or abolish it."*

Chapter 5

The Final Conversion—Horoscope Planet Numbers and Symbols into Astro (Sky) Carto (Maps) Graphy (That Can Be Read)

First a little history. The gestalt map view of the Earth, achieved by astrologers, did not exist before the late 1950s. When maps began to appear, the first conceptualizations were attributed to astrologers Roy C. Firebrace (1889-1974), Donald Bradley (1925-1974), Dr. Marc Edmund Jones (1880-1980), Cyril Fagan (1896-1970), Gary Duncan (1931-1988) and Jim S. Lewis (1941-1995) who independently, in the 1970s, took the giant technical steps, which transformed natal relocation astrology techniques into a world cartography map. Astro*Carto*Graphy® (A*C*G) was one of the greatest advancements in astrology in the Twentieth Century.

Relocation astrology theorizes that movement of an individual or nation's horoscope to a new location, and adjusting for time of day, allows different qualities contained within the horoscope's symbolism to be contacted, exercised and mastered around the Earth.

Gary Duncan was a computer programmer, who programmed for NASA and published one of the first-ever computer-generated Mundane maps in the 1966 *Llewellyn Moon Sign Book*. Also, in 1966, Cyril Fagan, practicing as a sideralist astrologer, described the mathematical methods and interpretive approaches in the January-February issue of *American Astrology* magazine.

I was one of three people in the room, in the autumn of 1988, when Matrix Software owner Michael Erlewine made his ground-breaking deal with Jim Lewis to convert Jim's Astro*Carto*Graphy® (A*C*G) into AstroMap® Hi-Res. I believe Erlewine provided professional astrologers with the ultimate tool. It certainly became the mainstay of my work for three decades.

The horoscopes and maps of this book are built on the backs of giants in the relocation astrology field. Now, through modern relocation map lens, an astrologer can look at the US horoscope, and address all manner of issues that should concern leadership of all countries. Where are the interests of a particular country geographically? What sort of borders do they have with what kinds of neighbors? Where do they need to go to trade to meet their economic requirements? Are they nations faced with geological conditions that are existential? In 2019 there are island nations confronted with Climate Change. The wolf is at their door now! Where can they go? What are their options in the international community?

Within my decades long published history of work I have demonstrated A*C*G offering *not on the map* perspectives on banking, hurricanes and military questions. Tease out a *WIP* for a country and consider what problem solving relationship it might reveal. The WIP is specific to US interests with respect to its military historical record. So what use can this such a map of reality be put towards, for a different country?

Astrology, Geopolitics & the *WIP*

An intelligent strategy for global military defensive positions, protection of waterways, supply lines, transportation routes, and the like have always been the sought-after advantage of nations. It has been the concern of their military men. For centuries military leaders of super powers have drawn up war plans against their competitors. Wars could involve borders, farmland, living space, strategic minerals, trade routes on land and water. Choke points on land and waterways were hotly contested by many nations. A field of study concerned with these issues evolved. It was labeled Geopolitics.

KEY WIP BRANCHES: 35° NORTH & SOUTH ~ 6° NORTH & SOUTH
10° EAST ~ 103° EAST ~ 77° WEST ~ 169° WEST ~ 3° WEST

Geopolitics is the study of how the geography of the Earth impacts political relationships between countries across the globe. Its masters were known as geostrategic thinkers or geostrategists. I have concluded that even with their great theories at hand, MacKinder's *Heartland Theory*, Mahan's *Debatable and Debated* zone and Spykman's *Rimland Theory*, clear intelligence as to *when* and *where* was inaccurate or lacking.

Over time the advantages of one nation over another could shift, perhaps because a technical innovation provided some temporary advantage. Temporary. How could a nation with poor physical assets survive its neighbors? When it is landlocked, in the face of endless challenges from neighbors, where does a nation grow its commerce? This was the puzzle that drove German geopolitics for centuries. A country could choose a military option to gain advantage over its neighbor.

Geopolitics is about military options, the different kinds and levels of warring against neighbors. It was 19th Century Prussian officer Carl von Clausewitz who famously defined war as, "An act of force to compel our enemy to do our will." America's trade war with China during 2019 is an example of this. Russia's vast heartland seemed the idea case of geopolitical advantage in Englishman MacKinder's eye. He saw that the great bear-sized nation could always hibernate, could suffer enormous losses, retreat into itself and regroup, as it did twice, once with Napoleon and again, a century later, with Hitler. America's Mahan saw the geography differently. He saw seapower and control of land and waterways between 30° and 40° degrees north as giving the advantage. It is curious to me that his zone was between 30° and 40° degrees North. Mahan advanced his theories in the early 1900s.

America's center of military power is situated at 35° North, exactly in the middle of Mahan's "Debatable and Debated" zone. The US, so far, has seemed impregnable, with two vast oceans protecting its three thousand mile wide heartland's east and west flanks. With America exploiting its wealth of long coastlines, harbors and waterways, Mahan saw how a blue water navy would equip the US with power to leverage far into the twentieth century. Mahan had a strong American president, Teddy Roosevelt, backing his ideas, executing on his theories, building a modern fleet. Under another Roosevelt, FDR, air and sea power was prioritized changing the balance of world power, in America's direction during and after WWII. Dominance in the air and on the seas assured

US hegemony across the Earth throughout the twentieth century. The **geology** of Earth does not shift, but human made **geographical** borders can.

The once great USSR has seen a great shrinking, casting off parts as multitudes of new nations. Fifteen new nations were formed. Is this temporary? There are levers to changing geographic-geological realities being pulled once again. In 2019, military struggles roil the stretches of Mahan's "Debatable and Debated" lands between 30° and 40° North latitudes. Places like Kabul, Afghanistan (34° North 31'31"); Irbil, Iraq (36° North 11'28"); Tehran, Iran (35° North 41'21"); Srinagar, Kashmir (34° North 5'24"); Tripoli, Libya (32° North 53'14"); Deir ez-Zor, Syria (35° North 20'). From Tripoli to Srinagar is over 3,600 miles. Superpowers are once more vying with regional powers for the key to advantage, for hegemony.

It is ironic to me that those great geopolitical thinkers, with their unusual theories, saw coastal communities, some part of the "Debatable and Debated" lands between 30° and 40° North Zone, and parts of a Spykman's heavily populated Rimland zone, as geography crucial to geopolitical advantage. Enter my WIP Theory, with its focus on specific major A*C*G lines to the far west and the far east of MacKinder's heartland and my 35° North Paran exactly aligned to today's and tomorrow's geopolitical concerns. The WIP extends the field of geopolitics. It provides the means to accurately map and measure *when* and *where*. Here are the maps.

Map 5. Four angular US Mars ♂ lines.

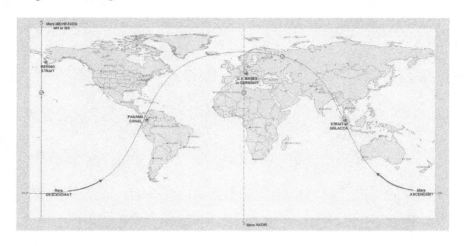

Map 6. Four angular US Uranus ♅ lines.

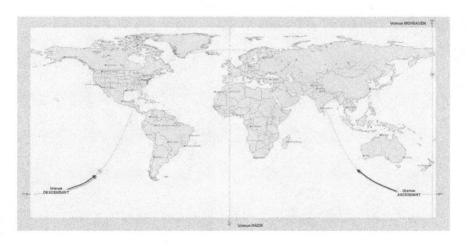

KEY WIP BRANCHES: 35° NORTH & SOUTH ~ 6° NORTH & SOUTH
10° EAST ~ 103° EAST ~ 77° WEST ~ 169° WEST ~ 3° WEST

MARS ♂ 21° GEMINI 22' ♂ URANUS ♅ 8° GEMINI 55' □ NEPTUNE ♆ 22° VIRGO 25'

Map 7. Four angular US Neptune ♆ lines.

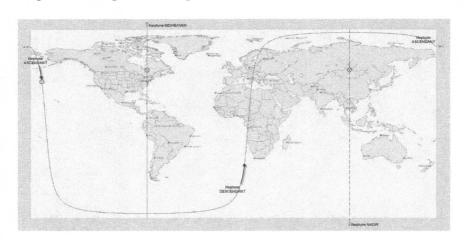

Map 8. Combined four angular Mars ♂, Uranus ♅ and Neptune ♆ lines, producing places of overlapping lines.

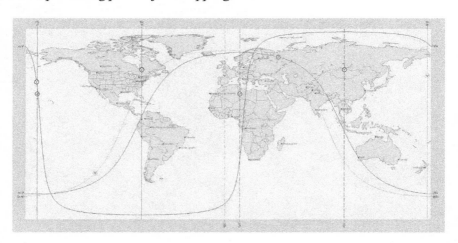

KEY WIP BRANCHES: 35° NORTH & SOUTH ~ 6° NORTH & SOUTH
10° EAST ~ 103° EAST ~ 77° WEST ~ 169° WEST ~ 3° WEST

The Parans in the *WIP*

This final and most complete picture of the *War Impulse Pattern (WIP)* is achieved on the map where four horizontal lines have drawn around the Earth through those places where the lines of the three angular planets cross or intersect. These lines are called Paranatellonta or Paran lines, for short. The ancient Paran was a situation where "Paranatellonta are stars or star groups that fall upon angles at the same time that a significant constellation or planet is also upon the angles."

Modern PARANS, were made popular on maps by astrology pioneer Jim Lewis. If the major planet lines can be likened to arteries and veins, the Parans—minor lines—are its minor blood vessels and capillaries reaching the most remote parts of a body. Parans describe a different *not on the map* reality that complements and details the narrative read in the ten major planet lines. Lewis proffered a modernized astrological perspective, where multiple planets can be simultaneously on the ASCENDANT—ASC, MIDHEAVEN—MH, DESCENDANT—DSC, or NADIR—IC angles. One can witness this firsthand by looking at the sky with the naked eye or through a horoscope during many commonly occurring moments.

Map 9. Combined Mars ♂, Uranus ♅ and Neptune ♆, with horizontal paran lines, running through the points of overlap.

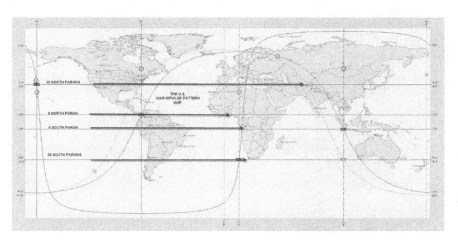

MARS ♂ 21° GEMINI 22' ♂ URANUS ♅ 8° GEMINI 55' □ NEPTUNE ♆ 22° VIRGO 25'

Map 10. 35° North Parans of WIP through areas conflict zones of 2019 involving US.

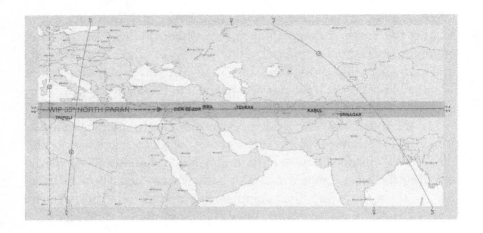

Horoscope 9. The horoscope's angles, where Parans are determined, are the beginnings of the 1st, 4th, 7th, and 10th houses.

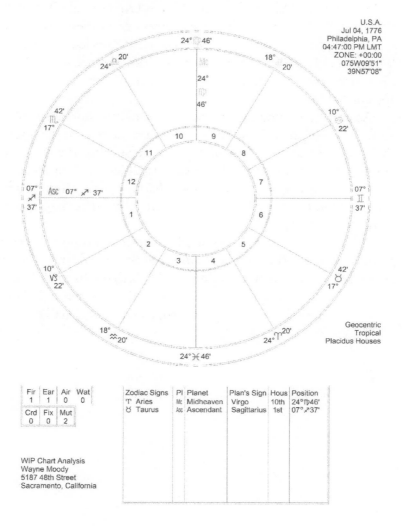

U.S.A.
Jul 04, 1776
Philadelphia, PA
04:47:00 PM LMT
ZONE: +00:00
075W09'51"
39N57'08"

Geocentric
Tropical
Placidus Houses

Fir	Ear	Air	Wat
1	1	0	0

Crd	Fix	Mut
0	0	2

Zodiac Signs	Pl	Planet	Plan's Sign	Hous	Position
♈ Aries	Mc	Midheaven	Virgo	10th	24°♍46'
♉ Taurus	Asc	Ascendant	Sagittarius	1st	07°♐37'

WIP Chart Analysis
Wayne Moody
5187 48th Street
Sacramento, California

©1994 Matrix Software Big Rapids, MI

Novice 2 Wheel

KEY WIP BRANCHES: 35° NORTH & SOUTH ~ 6° NORTH & SOUTH
10° EAST ~ 103° EAST ~ 77° WEST ~ 169° WEST ~ 3° WEST

The angles for the US horoscope are moving clockwise: the ASCENDANT (ASC) at 7° Sagittarius 37', the MIDHEAVEN (MH/Mc) at 24° Virgo 46', 7° Gemini 37' at the DESCENDANT (DSC), and a NADIR (IC), at 24° Pisces 46'. Whenever planets cross these points, relevant synchronicities play out. One does not need to calculate, just observe. We see the Moon and the Sun forming PARANS twice monthly between the eastern and western horizons with the top of the sky (the horoscope apex or MH).

As has been stated throughout this book, the horoscope of the US, set for Philadelphia, shows the planet Neptune next to the MIDHEAVEN (MH or Mc) to the right of the line separating the 9th and 10th houses. In the same two-dimensional depiction, Uranus is next to the DESCENDANT (DSC) angle, atop that line separating the sixth and seventh Houses of the horoscope. Again, this pattern in a horoscope constitutes a Paran.

The actual geographic point where both Neptune and Uranus are precisely angular is in North Carolina at 35° North 09'/76° West 56', near Grantsboro, North Carolina at 35° North 08'26"/76° West 50'33". That 35° North crossing latitude sweeps to the west through Fort Bragg, North Carolina. Here are the horoscope and map visuals.

Horoscope 10. The US Neptune in relationship to Uranus—both angular.

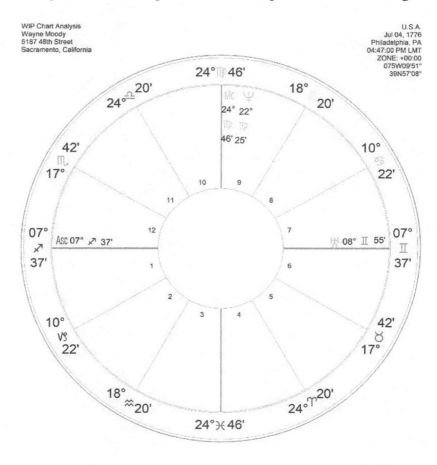

WIP Chart Analysis
Wayne Moody
5187 48th Street
Sacramento, California

U.S.A.
Jul 04, 1776
Philadelphia, PA
04:47:00 PM LMT
ZONE: +00:00
075W09'51"
39N57'08"

AFA2 chart style

KEY WIP BRANCHES: 35° NORTH & SOUTH ~ 6° NORTH & SOUTH
10° EAST ~ 103° EAST ~ 77° WEST ~ 169° WEST ~ 3° WEST

MARS ♂ 21° GEMINI 22' ♂ URANUS ♅ 8° GEMINI 55' □ NEPTUNE ♆ 22° VIRGO 25'

Map 11. Seen as a map, the 35° north branch of the WIP originates with where the PARAN of Uranus and Neptune is geographically exact.

Review what you know so far. The MIDHEAVEN (MH) corresponds to all descriptions and issues connecting to authority, power and leadership. The Descendant angle (DSC) represents the nation's relationships, compromises, and known enemies. The US was established in Philadelphia, Pennsylvania, on the principle of collective, democratic leadership of "We the People." Where Neptune and Uranus cross one another, collective (Neptune) freedom (Uranus) must rule the day, and innovative ideas concerning liberty must be a part of any governing, or the people rebel.

It bares repeating that geographically, this US Neptune/Uranus PARAN crossing line marks a place a few miles northwest of Grantsboro, North Carolina (35° North 08'26"). A line is a series of dots, joining to form the US *WIP* reality of connecting lines belting the Earth at *both* 6° North and South latitudes and *both* 35° North and South latitudes. The line's orb, or range of influence, stretches conservatively for a degree (sixty miles) north and south. However, in times of intensity, of waxing and precise planet transit contacts, timing synchronicities that belt's Neptune/Uranus expression can swell to twice the normal width creating a zone 240 miles or more in width.

Map 12. A wider map view of how the 35° North PARAN branch fits into the greater WIP.

When it does, it stretches from its baseline of 35° North, down south to 33° North, and up north to 37° North. This is very important when you consider that in easterly bearings 6,500 miles to the east of Fort Bragg, North Carolina, in Syria, Damascus is geographically at 33° North 30'47", Raqqah at 35° North 57', while Kobani is at 36° North 56'28". All three places are major conflict stages in the Syrian civil war. American Special Service *boots on the ground* are near or monitoring all these locations.

Here's a bit of trivia. Grantsboro, North Carolina, is home to Pepsi Cola. Pepsi is that innovative (Uranus) product that challenged and broke the Coca-Cola beverage dominance with their glamorous (Neptune) appeal to a "Pepsi Generation." This major cultural icon of the Twentieth Century is pure fad, pure glamour—resplendent and enticing in Neptune in attire. In another cultural curiosity, near Grantsboro is Bern, North Carolina, a place settled by Swiss and Palatine Germans. Throughout this WIP series, Germany will be shown to be historically an extremely important *WIP* connection. This German connection will be unpacked in forthcoming books.

There more, because of the *not on the map* astrology revelations. The eastern North Carolina geographic area of the US is arguably the most important nerve center, ground 0, of US military might on the US mainland. Within a radius of just over 2 degrees, or 145 miles, are historically and strategically most important American military bases, battlefields, historic places of innovation, naval bases, and forts. Within that circle are Fort Bragg, America's largest military base, Yorktown Battlefield National Park, Virginia; Norfolk, Naval Base and Shipyard, Virginia; Marine Corps Base Camp Lejeune, North Carolina; and Kitty Hawk National Park, North Carolina, where the miracle of manned flight took a giant leap.

In the next book of the *WIP* series, I will drill down deeper into this mesmerizing circle from the point of view of the US military forces moving forward in time.

Map 13. Concentration of US military history and power.

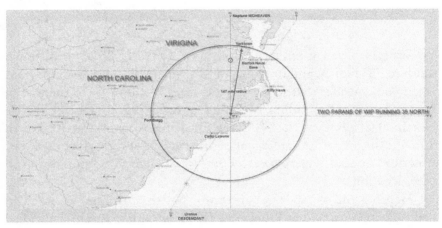

In summary, exercising the *WIP* foundational information given in this primer, one can see how far Mars, Uranus, and Neptune correspondences go toward ascribing meaning on the *when* and *where* and shed uncommon light upon the root causes for US battlefields of the past.

- Can that light be used today, turned to shine into the not-yet manifested future of the twenty-first century?
- Can vaulted human reasoning make that next great forward leap knowing the facts of today's conflict zones from the 24/7 news cycles?

KEY WIP BRANCHES: 35° NORTH & SOUTH ~ 6° NORTH & SOUTH
10° EAST ~ 103° EAST ~ 77° WEST ~ 169° WEST ~ 3° WEST

- Can the average American be educated to predict, before seeing them laid down on a map, where the US Mars, Uranus, and Neptune lines will geographically run? Is the ability to forecast *place* possible?
- Can we, using this tool, evolve to better divine *when*?

Postscript: America Judged as an Adult

We come to the end of this primer knowing certain things that were not previously on the map of conventional understanding.

- We know that we celebrate July 4, because the US came into existence in a Significant astrological moment.
- We know that the US horoscope, calculated as our nation's birth in 1776, becomes a tool, an awesome key to seeing things outside the understanding of conventional philosophies—things *not on the map*.
- We know that monitoring, researching, and watching historical events and stories, measured against that moment, synchronize with a pattern of three planets Mars, Uranus, and Neptune and can teach us a great deal.
- We know that the US has had significant stages of growth in its military prowess that can be measured against the cyclical astronomical-astrological Returns of Mars, Uranus, and Neptune.
- We have learned that even without an honest treatment of events (the victor's history), we can revisit past moments through their astrological facts and those certain hard facts of place and time, teasing out what was not on the map.

The stories told during the Returns of each of the three *WIP* planets provide us the language to understand them in terms of actions, intentions, issues, and values. We must refresh the stories, growing the narratives with new language whenever necessary. The descriptions and language we use grow a vocabulary around the three planets.

MARS ♂ 21° GEMINI 22' ♂ URANUS ♅ 8° GEMINI 55' □ NEPTUNE ♆ 22° VIRGO 25'

The US Constitution was a groundbreaking document flawed by the dealings of self-interested people over slavery and who had access to the franchise. The Civil War revealed serious flaws in the execution of the high ideals of equality of human beings espoused in the American Constitution. The reckoning for those flaws and omissions came fourscore and seven years, during America's first Uranus return. The first since the guiding creed was set down in the founding Declaration of Independence (DOI) document. The Civil War synchronized with the return of two of the three *WIP* planets, Mars and Uranus. The lesson is clear. Betray the stated ideals and face the congenital impulse for rebellion, a cornerstone of our country's beginning.

Certain returns have been stunning in what they synchronized. US airpower evolved under a Uranus branch of the WIP and became an American forte during the twentieth century. With the near simultaneous return of all three planets, in the mid-twentieth century (1938–1945), the US reached the pinnacle of its military power, using its airpower and assumed the mantle of reigning world super power. Leveraged by its mastery of the skies, the US grew to be master of space of Global Positioning System (GPS) technology. Not celebrated as important is the fact that the US GPS is geographically set in the teeth of the WIP, with ground stations situated on tiny specks of land in the midst of two vast oceans.

Map 14. *US GPS ground antenna locations in the WIP.*

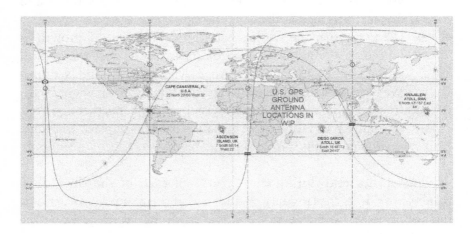

KEY WIP BRANCHES: 35° NORTH & SOUTH ~ 6° NORTH & SOUTH
10° EAST ~ 103° EAST ~ 77° WEST ~ 169° WEST ~ 3° WEST

America is now a fifth into the twenty-first century, only its fifth as a nation, a young adult nation in the community of some two hundred nations. Now as an adult, America is responsible for the exercise of its powers. Many of the older nations of the world have already reached and experienced critical crisis phases of development in their history the likes of which the US is currently experiencing. These things include environmental degradation, growing population pressures, need for jobs, challenges from enemies. Today's challenges, things like Climate Change, are of an unprecedented scale.

For the US, events that are *not on the map* in the public mind and major planet Returns, will synchronize significant transformations. Time is rapidly running down for the country's leaders to anticipate needs and make careful, appropriate plans for 2022. These plans should be commensurate with a season of great events great existential steps. America's first Pluto Return is exact on February 21, 2022. It should be noted that American style capitalism, inspired by Adam Smith's Wealth of Nations was published in March of 1776. America's economy is facing the same Pluto Return. Three different US Pluto A*C*G lines run within miles Beijing, China; Tehran, Iran; and Brazilia, Brazil. All these capitals will be involved in a script with the US. The US has major economic interests in all three nations, unprecedented tariffs against China, crushing sanctions on Iran and a favorite trade status with Brazil. What will be the status of these by 2022?

Slow moving astrology transits are pointing out the urgency of the situation, measuring tremendous events. The US has been in an economic and military standoff with China that has rocked international trade. The WIP's *not on the map* revelations about the militarization of islands in the South China Sea, should be cautionary warnings. Iran's military and US sanctions mix a deadly brew. All the military maneuvering in the Middle East and Persian Gulf invite kinetic events. Both situations resemble tinderboxes.

Again America's Pluto Return in February 2022, with a retrograding period around 27° Capricorn 34', with peak intensity lasting until October 2023. Synchronizing this retrograde period, will be two US Mars Returns, historically the 130th (April 9, 2021) and the 131st (October 4, 2022). Given the tense narrative playing out today, in 2019, these Returns will likely synchronize significant US/Iran military agitations all along 35° North latitude, running precisely through Tehran, Iran, a place just 85 miles from the epic transit activity of the US Pluto Mc line, at 50° East longitude, to the west.

KEY WIP BRANCHES: 35° NORTH & SOUTH ~ 6° NORTH & SOUTH
10° EAST ~ 103° EAST ~ 77° WEST ~ 169° WEST ~ 3° WEST

Map 15. *Concerning geography where the upcoming US Pluto Return will focus.*

Map 16. Where the US 35° North branch of the WIP crosses with US Pluto lines—great danger exists.

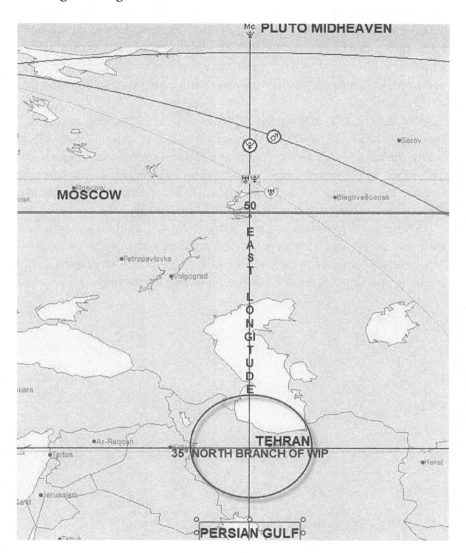

There is one sure thing we know about the *WIP* symbolism. We know that when the founding ideals are at the root of action for Americans, history shows the culture at its best. When existentially necessary action is taken by enlightened leaders, fair and balanced engagement can be entered upon with global partners. If a country had a tool that identified within a narrow geographic belt the battlefields and conflict zones of future wars, wouldn't that be valuable, strategic intelligence?

We now know that another planet will be returning in the US horoscope that has not been the subject of this primer. The US is facing the first ever return of Pluto to its astronomical-astrological–27° Capricorn 34'–position from July 4, 1776. The years prior to this epic Return are proving to be bellwethers, full of extraordinary events, impacting the US and the international community.

The leadership of our country needs to be sure-footed, using its best tools to address similarly experienced challenges from the past and if totally unprecedented manage them differently and with powerful and awesome intelligence from tools *not previously on the map*.

Bibliography

Banzhaf, H., *Tarot and the Journey of the Hero*. York Beach, Maine. Samuel Weiser, INC., 2000.

Bills, R. E., *The Rulership Book*. Tempe, AZ. American Federation of Astrologers, Inc., 1971.

Bobrick, B., *The Fated Sky: Astrology in History*. New York, NY. Simon & Schuster, 2005.

Campion, N., *The Book of World Horoscopes*. Bouremouth, UK. The Wessex Astrologer, 2004.

"Challenger STS 51-L Accident." National Aeronautics and Space Administration (January 28, 1986). http://history.nasa.gov/citeguide. html.

Clausewitz, C., *On War*. (Howard, M & Paret, P. Trans.). Germany: Alfred A. Knopf, 1993

Crane, S., *The Red Badge of Courage*. New York: Charles Scribner's Sons, 1895.

Erlewine, M. *AstroMap HiRes*. Big Rapids, MI: Astro*Talk Bulletin,1988.

Fact Sheet from BUREAU OF INTELLIGENCE AND RESEARCH. Retrieved January 20, 2017 from http://www.state.gov/r/pa/ei/rls/dos/436.htm.

Greene, L, *The Astrological Neptune and the Quest for Redemption*. Boston, MA: Weiser Books, 1996.

Greene, L, *The Outer Planets & Their Cycles-The Astrology of the Collective*. Reno, NV: CRCS Publicans, 1983.

Guttman and A. Lewis, J., *The Astro*Carto*Graphy Book of Maps: The Astrology of Relocation - How 136 Famous People Found Their Place*. St. Paul, MN. Llewellyn Publications, 1989.

Graphiq, (n.d.). Compare Branches of the US Military. *Inside Gov* (September 4, 2017). http://us-military-branches.insidegov.com.

Green, Raphael, Carter, *Mundane Astrology: The Astrology of Nations and States*. Bel Air, MD. Astrology Classics, 2004.

Michelsen, N, *The American Ephemeris for the 20th Century-1900 to 2000 at Noon*. San Diego, CA: ACS Publications, 1992.

Michelsen, N, *The American Ephemeris for the 21st Century-2001 to 2050 at Midnight*. San Diego, CA: ACS Publications, 1992.

Moody, W., *The Great Satan*. Eugene, OR. *Welcome to Planet Earth Journal. Vol. 7 No. 3.*, 1987.

Peak, D., *Synchronicity: The Bridge Between Matter and Mind*. New York, NY. Bantam Books, 1987.

Shapiro, F. R., *The Yale Book of Quotations*. New Haven and London. Yale University Press, 2006.

Sullivan, W., "The Einstein Papers. A Man of Many Parts." *New York Times* (March 23, 1972). http://www.nytimes.com/1972/03/29/

archives/the-einstein-papers-a-man-of-many-parts-the-einstein-papers-man-of.htm;?mcubz=1&mcubz=1.

"US Declaration of Independence," (para. 30), 1776.

US Department of State. Department Organization (2017). http://www.state.gov/r/pa/ei/rls/dos/436.htm.

Von Franz, M., *Time: Rhythm and Repose*. Lancashire, Great Britain. Thames and Hudson, 1978.

Abbreviations Used in Book

ASC	Ascendant
A*C*G	Astro*Carto*Graphy
DSC	Descendant
DOI	Declaration of Independence
DS	Direct Station
Ic	Nadir
ISIL	Islamic State of Iraq and the Levant
MH/Mc	Midheaven
FDR	Franklin Delano Roosevelt
RR	Rodden Rating
RS	Retrograde Station
SR	Stationary Retrograde
WIP	War Impulse Pattern

CPSIA information can be obtained
at www.ICGtesting.com
Printed in the USA
BVHW030943141119
563831BV00005B/69/P

9 781796 068931